RED PANNIERS

© John Scott-Morgan, Kirk Martin and Lightmoor Press 2008
Designed by Ian Pope
British Library Cataloguing-in-Publication Data. A catalogue record for this book is available from the British Library
ISBN 13 9781899889297

LIGHTMOOR PRESS
Unit 144B Lydney Trading Estate, Harbour Road, Lydney, Gloucestershire, GL15 5EJ
Lightmoor Press is an imprint of Black Dwarf Lightmoor Publications Ltd
Printed by Craft Print, Singapore

in association with

london
transport
museum

L89 (5775) in Neasden Yard during the summer of 1968.
Kirk Martin

RED PANNIERS

LAST STEAM ON THE UNDERGROUND

Red pannier L99 heads away from Lillie Bridge Depot through West Kensington station on the District Line circa 1970.   *Ron Head*

JOHN SCOTT-MORGAN
&
KIRK MARTIN

DEDICATION
To all the London Transport steam men
who worked on and maintained the thirteen red panniers from 1956 to 1971.

L94 stands at Watford Tip whilst the driver has a check round.   *Geoff Plumb*

L99 stands on Neasden Shed.

Mike Morant

CONTENTS

THE LAST OF THE PANNIERS

On seeing an ex-Great Western pannier tank locomotive on the London Underground. March 28th, 1968.

Between the darkness and the light
Where railway ghosts come into sight
There was a pannier passing by
In colours strange to Western eye.

Panting through those Stygian ways,
Far from Swindon's glorious days,
Gliding almost without sound –
A stranger on the Underground.

Shades of 'condensing tanks' long past –
With flashing cranks she whispered fast
(Along the District Line to die?)
Proud with smoke from chimney high.

Swiftly she steamed with fearless 'cough'
To warn electric fiends far off
In darkest tubes 'neath London's scene
That she was not 'a steam has-been.'

Her whistle shrieked the knell of steam,
And fast she faded as a dream;
Splendid, to, me, she passed and gave
A lasting vision beyond the grave!

A.S.C.

The entrance to Watford Tip   *Geoff Plumb*

The way I first remember them as a nine year old school boy at lunch time on my way back to school at Ealing Common. Often, while waiting for my District or Piccadilly line train, I would stand at the end of the platform and watch the smartly painted red pannier shunting the yard at Acton Works hoping it would run up the head shunt to give me a better view of her. L92 (5786) shunts a train of rail bogie flats in the winter of 1968. This locomotive is happily still with us as it was sold to the Worcester Locomotive Society after withdrawal in 1969. *Dr T. A. Gough*

INTRODUCTION
RED GHOSTS IN THE NIGHT

JOHN SCOTT-MORGAN

It normally happened around one in the morning. As I lay in bed half asleep there came like a dream, or a throw back to a recently passed age, the sound of a steam locomotive working hard up the bank from Acton Town station towards Ealing Common, past the looming form of the District car depot which had been built in 1905 in connection with the electrification of that line. The sound was that of an ex-Great Western '57XX' 0-6-0 pannier tank and it reverberated across the extensive junction between the lines taking the Piccadilly and the District to Hounslow West, Uxbridge and Ealing Broadway. Through the still of the night, and over the slumbering households of west London, the Swindon beat of the pannier would go on for what seemed a long time until it faded away, leaving once again the silence of the small hours.

London Transport's fleet of panniers were elusive creatures of the night that seemed to rarely venture out into the light of day and when they did they seemed to almost hide from public view. They were not the first London Transport steam locomotives that I ever encountered. It was around 1957 or 1958 that I saw one of the ex-District Railway 0-6-0 tanks, either L30 or L31, at Acton Town station standing in the District Line platform with a works train. I shall never forget my first sight of that dark maroon livery, lined in yellow and black, with its London Transport ownership emblazoned in gold on the side tanks.

The first of the panniers I ever encountered was only a chance glimpse, from the wheels up to its running plate, whilst descending into the tunnel on the Piccadilly Line near Barons Court. In 1963 I attended the Metropolitan Railway's centenary celebrations at Neasden with my brother. As our train of new 'A' stock arrived at Neasden we passed the old Metropolitan Railway power station which stood behind the 1930s built London Transport steam shed, around which a large part of the pannier fleet were standing.

In all there were thirteen panniers owned by London Transport between 1957 and 1971 but not all of them ran together at the same time. The first L90 and L91 were exchanged by British Railways Western Region for two replacements in better condition and the last additions to the fleet were L89 and L99 in 1963. Members of the fleet could normally be found at Neasden or Lillie Bridge Depots, places that were hard to get to for most enthusiasts as they were either cut off within a large engineering facility as at Lillie Bridge or in close proximity to electrified running lines as at Neasden.

In the mid 1960s I used to commute to school from Acton Town to Ealing Common and on several occasions came across panniers on daily shunts at Acton Works which necessitated using the head shunts at Acton Town station. This was a good

Each a glimpse… Four views taken at West Kensington station of L99 (7715) passing through bunker first, having just left Lillie Bridge Depot, towards Barons Court. Passengers standing on the eastbound platform at West Kensington stand back and glance up from their newspapers as the pannier comes storming through the station wrong line before taking the crossover to gain the westbound rails.   *Adrian Garner*

... and gone for ever.

L98 (7739) makes a furtive dash past the camera on a train of empty rail flats near Harrow on the Hill in the summer of 1967. Its vapour leaving a white trail on its way to Neasden Yard.

photographer unknown

place to have a look at these rarely seen red beasts. There was also one occasion when one ran through Ealing Common station with a long train of 16-ton steel mineral wagons heading for Acton Town. I just missed the locomotive as I stood at the bottom of the steps leading from the booking hall watching the train disappearing in front of me.

At that time it made sense for London Transport to retain a fleet of steam locomotives for works trains as it was cheaper and more economic than purchasing a batch of diesels to do the same work, although a member of senior management seemed to 'have it in for' the small steam fleet by the early 1970s. A reliable source has told me the manager concerned said at the time of the final withdrawal of the last panniers in June 1971 'Thank God we have got rid of those steam locomotives'. He was concerned about the public image of London Transport still having a fleet of steam locomotives in 1971. There were still plenty of spare parts and the panniers were in reasonably good condition and could have continued in traffic for a few years more.

At the end of the day six out of the thirteen locomotives have been saved for preservation, almost half the London Transport fleet, and that is quite an achievement.

An unidentified pannier stands on the coal stage at Neasden c1965. Note that the line into the shed has been blocked off for some reason.

J. E. Connor

CHAPTER ONE
ORIGINS OF THE '57XX' PANNIER TANKS

The '57XX' 0-6-0 pannier tank was a product of Great Western Railway locomotive evolution and of that company's standardisation policy which was fully implemented during the tenure of George Jackson Churchward as Chief Mechanical Engineer at the start of the 20th century. The GWR had, at that period, a large number of 0-6-0 saddle tank classes, of both heavy and light weight types, dating from the 1870s, some being conversions from broad gauge machines. They also originated from a variety of builders in addition to the Great Western's own works at Swindon and Wolverhampton.

The first panniers appeared on the Great Western in 1904 when some of the '2021' class saddle tanks were rebuilt with pannier tanks. The reason for the change from saddle tank over the top of the boiler to the panniers on either side was the introduction of the Belpaire boiler. First introduced on the GWR in the late 1890s it had a flat square top and was raised up from the boiler thus making it impractical for use with a saddle tank.

Gradually all of the saddle tanks were rebuilt as panniers as they went through the works for major overhaul and were fitted with the new boiler and firebox. The pannier tank was a design almost unique to the Great Western. An advantage of the tank position, over the more normal side tank mounted on the footplate, was that it gave better access to the inside motion.

Thus the old saddle tanks with their mixed origins continued to give good service but were aging. The inheritance by the Great Western of a large number of 'non standard' tank locomotives at the grouping in 1923 and the need to replace a large number

of them led to the design of a new standard tank locomotive and so the '57XX' class was conceived. That being said its true origins were the '2721' class of 0-6-0 saddle tanks built between 1897 and 1901. There were a total of eighty in the class and they were built with 4ft 7$\frac{1}{2}$in. driving wheels and had been rebuilt with pannier tanks.

The first examples of the '57XX' appeared in 1929 to the design of Charles B. Collett who had taken over from Churchward in 1921. These sturdy, well designed and powerful tank locomotives proved a great success on all the work they were employed on. Over a period of twenty years 863 examples were constructed, many by outside builders; Armstrong Whitworth, W. & G. Bagnall, Beyer Peacock, Kerr Stuart, North British and the Yorkshire Engine Company all contributing to the total. In all a quarter of the class were constructed by outside builders.

There were two distinct outward design features of the class, in that the early members had a square Churchward style cab and the later batches had a round top Collett style cab. The earlier examples were slightly narrower in the beam than the later examples and thus were the ones from which the London Transport fleet were selected. One further design variant was to be found in the examples that made up the eleven '9701' condensing locomotives built in 1931 to work meat trains to Smithfield Market over the northern part of the Circle Line. This traffic continued until the early 1960s. To fit the condensing gear the panniers had to be cut back short of the smokebox. '57XX' number 8700 was so adapted but in trials water was found to

5775 (later L89) at Pontypool Road in 1961, a fine study of a '57XX' pannier when at work on British Railways. *J. Davenport/Initial Photographics*

Charles B. Collett: CME Great Western Railway 1922-1941
With his team at Swindon he was responsible for designing the 57XX pannier tanks in 1929.
John Chacksfield collection

be in short supply so the class were built with extensions to the panniers making them a hybrid side/pannier tank.

The dimensions of the '57XX' pannier class were: driving wheels 4ft 7½in.; length 31ft 2in.; weight 50 tons; water capacity 1,200 gallons; cylinders 17½in. x 24in.; boiler pressure 200lbs per square inch; tractive effort 22,515lbs; coal capacity 3 tons 6 cwt; route availability yellow; GWR power class 'C'.

The purpose of this type was originally for shunting and light freight work. However, they were soon found on everything from suburban passenger and pilot work to hauling quite heavy freight trains. Almost every major Great Western shed had a number of examples and in some areas like South Wales and most major cities served by the Great Western one could find large numbers allocated to depots.

The various number series of the overall type ran as follows: 5700 – 5799; 6700 – 6779; 7700 – 7799; 8700 – 8799; 9701 – 9799, 3600 – 3699, 3700 – 3799, 4600 – 4699, 9600 – 9682. It should be added that 6700 – 6779 were not vacuum fitted.

The final development of the Great Western 0-6-0 pannier tanks were designed by F. W. Hawksworth who introduced three classes to the Great Western and the Western Region of British Railways. These were the '94XX' in 1947, the '15XX' with outside cylinders in 1949 and the '16XX', also in 1949, to replace the last surviving 1901 and 2021 class panniers built at the end of the 19th century.

The Underground had a long association with the Great Western which dated back to the opening of the Metropolitan Railway in 1863 when the Great Western provided the locomotives and carriage stock for the new company to run its early train services. In a strange twist of fate it was somehow historically appropriate that the last steam locomotives owned by London Transport running on the Underground should be of Great Western origin. The story had indeed come full circle!

7749 (L97) at Bristol Barrow Road shed.

J. Davenport / Initial Photographics

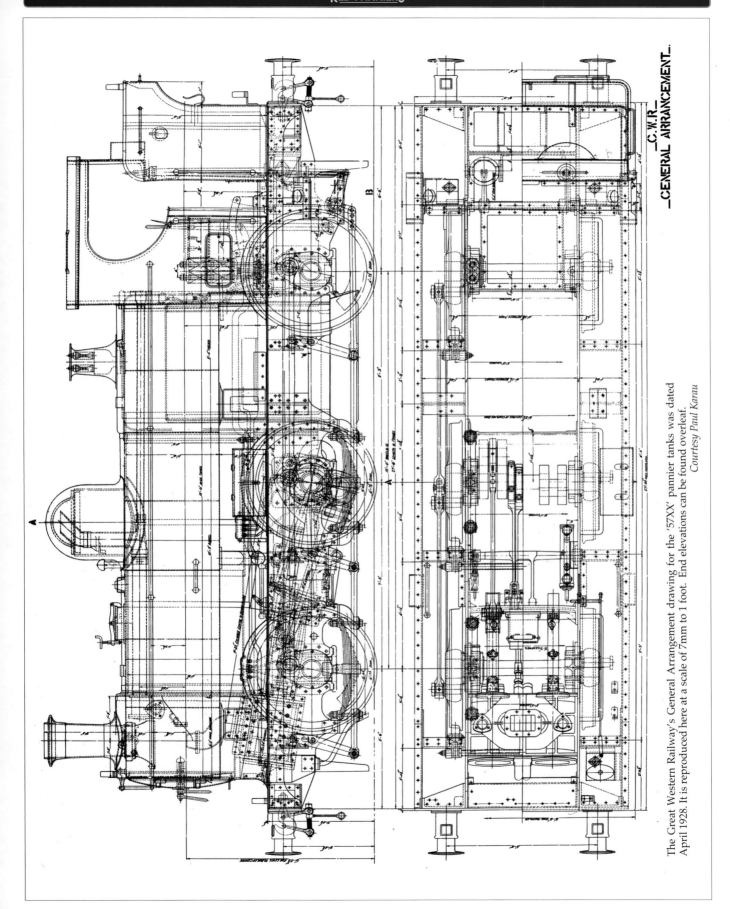

C.W.R.

GENERAL ARRANGEMENT.

The Great Western Railway's General Arrangement drawing for the '57XX' pannier tanks was dated April 1928. It is reproduced here at a scale of 7mm to 1 foot. End elevations can be found overleaf.

Courtesy Paul Karau

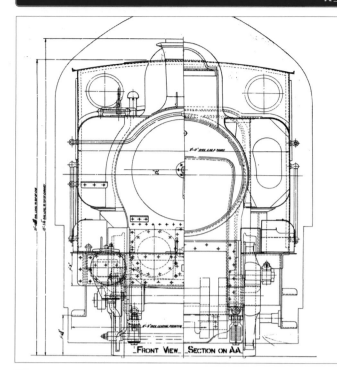

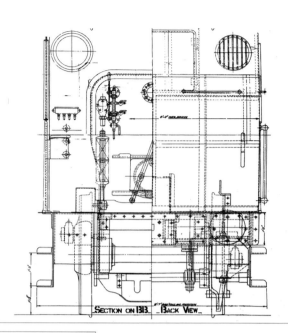

7715 (L99) at Lostwithiel station in July 1957 with a ballast train pre-empting its future career on London Transport when it would often be seen on such workings.

J. Davenport / Initial Photographics

7760 (the second L90) at Fairford with a local service on the 18th April 1960 only shortly before being sold to London Transport.

R. K. Blencowe collection

CHAPTER TWO
BEFORE THE RED PANNIERS

The Metropolitan Railway and the District Railway were originally operated solely by steam locomotives, both railways having fleets of Beyer Peacock 4-4-0 tank engines. In the case of the Metropolitan there were sixty-six, divided into two classes 'A' and 'B', whilst the District had fifty-four.

In 1905 the Metropolitan Railway south of Harrow and the District and Circle lines were electrified for passenger services but there still remained a need for a small number of steam locomotives for use on ballast and engineering trains. The District retained six whilst the Metropolitan kept thirteen beyond 1913, the majority having gone between 1905 and 1907 being sold off for further use elsewhere. The thirteen were further reduced with disposals in the 1920s: five in 1925 (one of which went to the District Railway), one in 1926, and two in 1928. This left five, numbers 23, 27, 41, 48 and 49 retained for use on the Brill Branch and, following closure of the branch in 1935 all bar number 23 were withdrawn. Number 23 became L45 and survived until withdrawal in 1948 for preservation.

The Metropolitan had always had a larger steam fleet to operate its more intensive goods services as well as passenger work. Prior to electrification more modern locomotives had been acquired. Four 'C' class 0-4-4 tanks were obtained in 1891 in readiness for the extension of services to Aylesbury in 1892 which gave the Met a main line of 38 miles to Baker Street. Six 'D' class 2-4-0 tanks were bought in 1894-5 for use on the ex-Aylesbury & Buckingham Railway lines to Verney Junction and the Brill Branch. Increasing traffic from Aylesbury led to the

acquisition of seven 'E' class 0-4-4 tanks between 1896 and 1901, the first three being built at Neasden. Two Peckett 0-6-0 saddle tanks were bought for shunting at Neasden and Finchley Road, the first in 1897 and the second two years later. Finally four 'F' class 0-6-2 tanks were bought in 1901 primarily for use on goods services to Aylesbury.

Goods traffic continued to grow and expanded beyond the capability of the 'F' class locomotives and so in 1915-16 four more powerful 0-6-4 tanks were acquired and these became the 'G' class.

The foreseen growth of 'Metro-Land' and the need for an improved and accelerated passenger service into the city led to the purchase of faster and more powerful passenger locomotives and so eight 'H' class 4-4-4 tanks were obtained in 1920-21. The final locomotive purchases by the Metropolitan were six 'K' class 2-6-4 tanks in 1925, again to deal with increasing goods traffic and also to allow for the electrification to Rickmansworth by the running of longer and faster goods trains. The larger locomotives acquired during and after the First World War allowed the older 'E' and 'F' class engines to be cascaded to the engineers' trains and lesser services whilst all of the Metropolitan's 'C' and 'D' class locomotives were sold off or scrapped between 1916 and 1923.

On the District, of the six Beyer Peacock 4-4-0s retained only two were still serviceable by 1909 and they were used for shunting at Lillie Bridge Depot. One of them was scrapped in 1925 and replaced by one of the Metropolitan's 4-4-0s. With

District Railway Beyer Peacock 4-4-0 tank number 34 at Lillie Bridge Depot with the cutting of the West London Line in the background c1910. Number 34 was one of six Beyer Peacock tanks retained by the District Railway after electrification in 1905 for further service on ballast and works trains. This locomotive was the last District 4-4-0 tank, withdrawn in 1928.
Kidderminster Railway Museum

their increasing age the District obtained two 0-6-0 tanks from Hunslet in 1931 which allowed the older locomotives to be withdrawn. The two Hunslets became the first locomotives to carry the 'L' prefix to their numbers, becoming L30 and L31.

In 1933 the District and the Metropolitan locomotives came under common management with the formation of the London Passenger Transport Board. In 1935 the first three of the 'E' class 0-4-4s were withdrawn.

In 1937 the operation of the Metropolitan line north of Rickmansworth was taken over by agreement by the London & North Eastern Railway. To enable them to do this the larger tank locomotives, the 'G', 'H' and 'K' classes were handed over to the LNER, together with the majority of the goods wagon fleet so that the latter company could maintain the goods services. The transfer of the locomotives enabled the demolition of the old Metropolitan steam shed to make way for new electric train sheds. To house the few Metropolitan locomotives which remained a new two-road shed was constructed. From 1937 onwards steam locomotives would be used in the main on ballast and engineers' trains. There would, however, be a need at certain times to use the locomotives of the 'E' and 'F' classes on passenger trains north of Rickmansworth, in order to assist the LNER, who operated the Metropolitan services to Aylesbury. They also worked on occasions to Quainton Road to provide a wartime passenger service for munitions workers who lived at Quainton and worked in Aylesbury. This continued until 1946.

Until 1937 the Metropolitan locomotives had, in the main, remain based on their home territory at Neasden. However, after that date a new operating pattern emerged with class 'E' and 'F' locomotives visiting and being allocated to Lillie Bridge Depot on the District Line, which also had an allocation of the two ex-District Railway Hunslet 0-6-0Ts, L30 and L31. This pattern continued through World War Two and into the post-war era until the mid 1950s when it became apparent that both the 'E' and 'F' classes were clearly past their prime. During the years from 1937 to 1955 the 'E' and 'F' class locomotives had worked hard and this had taken its toll on these small robust and powerful tank locomotives, especially during the war when they had worked long hours with little maintenance. A memo dated the 4th April 1955 draws attention to the need for extensive repairs to 'F' class L50 and also questions the future of the locomotive.

Even though the London Passenger Transport Board had divested itself of freight traffic in 1937 a certain obligation to this traffic still existed until the mid 1960s. This was in the form of coal traffic to various goods yards on the former Metropolitan Railway between Finchley Road and Amersham including the Watford and Uxbridge branches and also the gas works at South Harrow, which required some unusual shunting procedures involving propelling wagons from Rayners Lane station.

The on going cost of repairing old locomotives that were past their prime and the planned engineering project in the mid 1950s to quadruple the Metropolitan Main Line from Northwood to Moor Park in order to ease traffic problems, also required a fleet of service locomotives that were reliable and in good condition. Clearly the old Metropolitan locomotives were not up to the job and therefore a new approach was needed. London Transport had experimented with a diesel locomotive built to 'tube' loading gauge in the late 1930s. This machine, DEL120, lasted until 1958 and spent most of its time in store at Acton Works after use for a while on engineers' trains on the Central Line's eastern extension. It was not a great success and was finally withdrawn for scrap.

District Railway 0-6-0 tank L30, together with sister engine L31, were built in 1931 by Hunslet of Leeds to an industrial design and fitted with outside Walschaerts valve gear. They replaced the last Beyer Peacock 4-4-0 tank locomotives in service and, in turn, when both were withdrawn in 1963 they were replaced by panniers L89 (5775) and L99 (7715).
Ben Pope collection

Metropolitan 'A' Class 4-4-0 tank number 27 at Neasden shed c1921. Built by Beyer Peacock in 1867 for use on the Circle Line and services through to Harrow on the Hill. Like the District 4-4-0 tanks these locomotives were rendered redundant after the electrification of the Circle and the District lines in 1905. For a time, until the 1920s, they found alternative work on the line north of Harrow on the Hill hauling trains to Aylesbury and Verney Junction. These 'A' class tanks were rebuilt in the early years of the twentieth century by J. J. Hanbury as a result of which they were retained for use on the Brill Tramway and on engineers' trains. The 'B' class 4-4-0 tanks were not rebuilt and were all withdrawn in 1919. *R. C. Stumpf collection*

Metropolitan 'E' class, number 1, later L44 c1921 at Neasden shed. This locomotive is now preserved at the Buckinghamshire Railway Centre at Quainton Road. It was saved for preservation in 1963 by the London Railway Preservation Society. Number 1 was the last locomotive built at Neasden Works in 1898, taking its number from a withdrawn 'A' class 4-4-0 tank which had been involved in an accident. After 1937 these locomotives were used on ballast and engineers' trains on the former District and Metropolitan systems until replaced by the red panniers from 1956. *R. C. Stumpf collection*

'F' class 0-6-2T number 93, later L52, seen shunting at Neasden c1921. These locomotives were originally used on freight service on the lines north of Finchley Road to Verney Junction but were later cascaded on to ballast and engineers' trains in London Transport days. Like the 'E' class the 'Fs' were also used on the former District and Metropolitan lines on works trains until replaced by the panniers. *R. C. Stumpf collection*

Peckett 0-6-0 saddle tank number 101, built in 1897, was one of two locomotives of this type (the other, numbered 102, was built in 1899) used on shunting at Neasden and at Finchley Road goods yard where the Metropolitan Railway and the Midland Railway had an agreement to shunt the goods yard on alternate five year intervals. Both became London Transport locomotives: 101 becoming L53 and 102 becoming L54. They were withdrawn in 1960 and 1961 respectively. Number 101 is here seen at Neasden c1921.

R. C. Stumpf collection

'G' class 0-6-4 tank number 95 *Robert H Selbie* named after the Metropolitan Railway's general manager. Built by the Yorkshire Engine Company in 1915 and one of four members of its class. This locomotive was handed over to the LNER in 1937 and was later transferred to Leicester. Here seen at Neasden c1921.

R. C. Stumpf collection

'H' class 4-4-4 tank number 110 seen at Neasden Yard c1921 in ex-works condition. Built by Kerr Stuart in that year these handsome tanks were the mainstay of the Metropolitan's fast train service to Verney Junction north of Aylesbury. These locomotives were also handed over to the LNER in 1937, gravitating north to Leicester in the early 1940s.

R. C. Stumpf collection

'K' class 2-6-4 tank number 114 at Neasden shed c1925. These handsome 2-6-4 tanks were built using Woolwich Arsenal manufactured parts for the SECR 'N' class 2-6-0 tender locomotives. Redesigned into a 2-6-4 tank not dissimilar to the Southern 'River' class locomotives but unlike the ill fated 'River' tanks the Metropolitan 'K' class had a longer career being used on freight and passenger traffic. Built in 1925 by Armstrong Whitworth & Co. these locomotives were handed over to the LNER in 1937. They were initially used on the suburban services out of Marylebone to Aylesbury. The last members of the class were not withdrawn until 1948.

R. C. Stumpf collection

The experimental bogie diesel locomotive DEL120 at Lillie Bridge Depot on the 22nd June 1946. This locomotive was built in 1942 to tube loading gauge in order to evaluate the use of diesel traction on works trains. It was not a success being withdrawn on the 1st July 1958. Note the fully lined out body of a similar style to the steam locomotives of the time.

Reg Carter collection

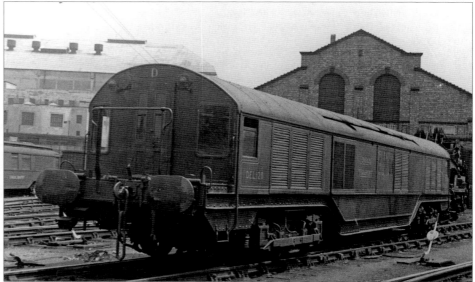

Battery locomotive L37 at Lillie Bridge, probably on the 17th September 1951. This example was built by the Gloucester Railway Carriage & Wagon Co. in 1938. It formed part of a batch of nine locomotives, specifically designed for such work. At the time of the purchase of the last panniers in 1963 there was much debate over the use of battery locomotives of this type in the future to replace the steam fleet.

Lens of Sutton Association

A memorandum dated the 22nd December 1953 from A. W. Manser, the Chief Mechanical Engineer, London Transport, to G. S. Bingham his assistant CME outlines the idea of replacing the steam fleet with a batch of British Railways standard 350 horsepower diesel electric shunting locomotives. A follow up memo dated 10th April 1954 from A. W. Manser to C. E. Dutton, also in the CMEs department at 55 Broadway further probes the question of replacing an 'F' class 0-6-2T, which was in need of a new boiler and firebox at a cost of £3,500, with a 350 horsepower diesel shunter. Manser asks if Dutton could look into the economic and operational value of such a move.

The idea of replacing steam was raised again in a further memo from L. R. Cotton, Divisional Depot Engineer 'A' Acton, dated the 23rd April 1954, when a breakdown of costs relating to trades required to maintain steam locomotives at Lillie Bridge Depot was discussed outlining possible redundancies of one engine fitter, one boiler maker, one coppersmith and two members of staff at Grade S/S2. Also, it was envisaged that one mechanical fitter lathe operator and a welder could be made redundant.

By the 30th April 1954, Manser was openly discussing all steam overhaul work at Lillie Bridge Depot with G. S. Bingham with a view to reducing the skilled steam maintenance staff by six, he was also discussing the proposal to replace all steam maintenance staff if London Transport went over to diesel traction.

The question of the 'F' class 0-6-2T, L51, which was due for a new boiler and firebox in 1956, was raised in a memo from Bingham dated the 12th February 1955, with a view to obtaining authority to order a new boiler and firebox from a manufacturer in view of no firm commitment having been made to the replacement of steam at that time. The memo also drew attention to the fact that the five other ex-Metropolitan locomotives would probably require new boilers between 1957 and 1961.

A follow up communication from Dutton to Manser, dated the 25th February 1955, refers to the possibility of replacing the boiler of 'F' class 0-6-2T L51 at a cost of £2,000, its present boiler dating from 1919 and its firebox renewal having been carried out in 1932. The boiler renewal would allow time to replace the steam fleet with a suitable type of diesel locomotive that would be able to haul ballast and works trains at 25 miles per hour with a heavy load. It was envisaged by some of the engineers on London Transport that it would take at least five years to design a suitable diesel locomotive for LT use.

There were in depth negotiations going on between London Transport and British Railways over this matter during 1955 with a view to obtaining a standard type of locomotive for use by both railways. A concern was raised over making the new diesel locomotive as silent as possible for night time use but it was pointed out that the existing steam locomotives were quite noisy, especially when heard from above Baker Street at night and this was not, therefore, a great concern.

A one page report dated the 4th April 1955 (right) to L. R. Cotton outlines the work that needed to be done on 'F' class locomotive L50. This was backed up by a one page report on the same date which outlines the hours worked by each locomotive and also refers to footplate crews' hours being worked on each locomotive.

At this stage it must have been of some concern that time was running out for the boilers of all the ex-Metropolitan locomotive fleet more or less at the same time without a replacement being readily available. It is not surprising that London Transport was trying to find a solution to a thorny question. However, it is quite surprising to look at the direction they initially went, for in a memo dated the 20th June 1955 we first find a proposal for a loan from British Railways Eastern Region of an old ex-Great Northern Railway J52 0-6-0 saddle tank, number 68862, designed in the 1880s by Patrick Stirling. This truly Victorian relic was much older than any of the Metropolitan locomotives it was meant to replace.

STEAM LOCOMOTIVE NO: L.50.

The above locomotive is at present being overhauled at Lillie Bridge and it has been found that extensive repairs are now necessary, particularly on the boiler and firebox. This, as you are aware, is scheduled for renewal in 1958.

I have examined this locomotive and find the following work will be necessary at this stage.

(1)   A large section of the firebox adjacent to the firing position will have to be renewed by patching.

(2)   The tube plate which has been previously built up by welding now requires renewal.

(3)   The steam chest wall of the cylinders has eroded leaving a section weak and we are hoping to make a satisfactory repair to last until the next overhaul period by fixing a plate, but these cylinders will definitely require renewal at the next overhaul.

(4)   The existing coupled axleboxes are generally worn but we anticipate that they will be serviceable until the next overhaul.

(5)   The main frames have patches over fractures at the driving end positions which have been built up at the expansion bracket positions.

(6)   The auxiliary reservoir and pipes connecting with the Westinghouse brake, and which are located under the bunker, have become very badly eroded due to the action of the steam and the reservoir is now completely scrap. This was fitted 5 years ago during its previous overhaul and once in position is quite inaccessible for any treatment or examination and I am concerned, in view of the internal pressure on these reservoirs, that they are no longer safe and, in fact, have been allowed to remain in their present position for so long as 5 years. The reservoir is at present at Lillie Bridge and perhaps you would care to see it during your next visit.

In view of my previous remarks regarding the locomotive generally, I would recommend that some consideration be given to its replacement before its next overhaul which is likely to be very expensive. The present overhaul will undoubtedly be a costly business from a labour point of view but I feel that we shall make it serviceable for sufficient time to justify the expense.

The memorandum of the 4th April 1955 from Percy Silverlock to L. R. Cotton regarding the condition of L50.
Transport for London Group Archives, LT254/1828

STEAM LOCOMOTIVES - USE IN SERVICE

An investigation has now been made into the working of steam locomotives, and the following is an analysis of the results which deal with the month of February.

The hours shown are those during which a driver was in charge of a particular locomotive, they are not hours during which the locomotives were actually performing a job of work. *

The maximum number of hours possible per locomotive for the four-weekly period is 672; the actual number of hours a driver was in charge of the locomotives is as follows:-

L.30	274 hours
L.31	320 "
L.44	155 "
L.46	165½ "
L.48	80½ "
L.49	369 "
L.50	323 "
L.51	296 "
L.52	282 "
L.53	In general overhaul
L.54	256 hours

The average for the 11 locomotives is 229 hours.

The hours during which a locomotive is actually performing useful work are difficult to obtain, but the following hours have been taken from the drivers' tickets for the 3 locomotives working at Lillie Bridge. These hours should be treated with a certain amount of reserve as they are probably less than the drivers have stated.

L.54	Hours driver in charge	- 256
	Hours actually worked by locomotive	- 173
L.30	Hours driver in charge	- 274
	Hours actually worked by locomotive	- 209½
L.31	Hours driver in charge	- 320
	Hours actually worked by locomotive	- 273

AFC/DR.

* The hours include preparation time and a large amount of time when the engine is brought back to the shed because there is no actual work to be done during a particular driver's shift.

The breakdown of locomotive hours produced in April 1955.
Transport for London Group Archives, LT254/1828

An example of a J52 showing what might have been. Photographs of the actual engine, 68862, which was to have been loaned have proved impossible to find. The height of the cab spectacles, occasioned by the position of the top of the saddle tank, is also apparent and it was thought that this would have led to signal sighting difficulties if it had ever ventured into the tunnels. However, one of the defects on the locomotive supplied led to its early return to BR – a leak in the saddle tank was flooding the footplate.

Lens of Sutton Association

ASSISTANT MECHANICAL ENGINEER (RUNNING)   A. W. MANSER ESQ.

L.12/   6th December 1955

BOILER REPLACEMENT PROGRAMME   691384
STEAM LOCOMOTIVES

Ex G.N.R. J.52 class 0-6-0 tank locomotive No. 68862 was received at Neasden Depot on the 30th September 1955 and by our standards was not in a very satisfactory condition, in addition to being extremely dirty.

The following parts were in our opinion defective -

1) Leading buffer beam was bent and the rivets to frames in both right and left hand gussets were sheared.

2) The right hand rear end of water tank was leaking badly due to defective structural welding.

3) The outside sections of spring links were worn by rubbing against the tyres.

4) The joint of the main safety valve casting to the boiler was leaking.

The engine was cleaned and tested in steam and apart from the above mentioned defects was passed fit for trial after the fitting of vacuum type trip cocks to the leading and trailing positions. After 24 hours working as a shunting engine it was withdrawn as the leak from the water tank above mentioned had worsened until the cab floor became extremely wet.

The repair to the water tank is of a major character, involving removal of most of the engine superstructure. The engine is therefore stopped.

Some complaint was also received from the Operating Department that the sighting of signals in tunnel working would be extremely difficult with this class of engine as the spectacles are set too high because of the position of the water tanks.

I have given instructions for the trip cocks to be removed and the engine to be returned to the Eastern Region.

I think the receipt of this engine for trial has been of value if only to emphasize the high standard in which our own engines are maintained and I could only look upon the displacement of our present engines by the J.52 class as being a retrograde step.

Continued

Perhaps you will let me know the next move in regard to this engine, and the action to be taken in regard to procuring a replacement boiler for our 'F' class engine No. L.51 which is due for overhaul in 1956.

I still think as a general long term policy the replacement of our engines by a suitable engine standard to British Railways should be pursued, and in this connection could we not obtain details of the Western Region 0-6-0 saddle tanks which in view of recent new additions to the class appear to be an accepted standard for many years to come.

I attach all relevant papers regarding the J.52 engine.

The report on the J52 which shows that the locomotive sent by BR was not in the best of condition, the four main faults being the bent leading buffer beam, leaking tank, worn spring links and leaking safety valve joint. *Transport for London Group Archives, LT254/1828*

A report produced on the J52 showed that the locomotive had a long list of defects and it is a wonder, knowing the high standard of London Transport engineering and the pride with which LT ran its operation, that BR Eastern Region ever dispatched a locomotive in the state that this example was in. The J52 further disgraced itself during trials on the 17th November 1955, as a memo from L. R. Cotton points out, it was suffering from a leak in the saddle tank as well as leaking water cocks in the cab. The locomotive was withdrawn and instructions requested as to what to do next.

The J52 was sent home after the problems were encountered on the 17th November and this led to some new avenues being considered. Quite apart from the poor condition of 68862, there were concerns about visibility through the cab windows towards the front and back of the locomotive and also the need to modify boiler fittings and its chimney so the locomotive could fit in the tunnels. This would have required fitting the locomotive with a short chimney and also a dome cover of reduced height. It would also have meant the possibility of having to reduce the cab profile all of which would have taken time and increased the cost.

The situation must have been getting desperate, as London Transport found themselves considering an ex-Royal Ordinance Factory tank engine locomotive built in 1946 by Bagnall, works number 37/1808 type one. No wheel arrangement is referred to in a letter dated the 5th April 1955 but its condition was said to be 'fair'. This locomotive was soon turned down as being unsuitable.

It was at this stage that developments started to turn in a new direction and thoughts began to focus on an alternative solution to this pressing problem. After 52 years it is hard to pinpoint the reasoning behind the decision to borrow an ex-Great Western '57XX' pannier tank for trials, but it has been pointed out by a reliable source of information that during the construction of the Central Line extension from North Acton to West Ruislip in the late 1940s, Great Western pannier tanks, mostly of the '57XX' series, worked the engineers and spoil trains along the formation. These engines were working out of Old Oak Common shed and yard. Perhaps there were some people within London Transport who recalled how efficient and useful these locomotives had been, and that there was no harm in giving an example of this well designed class a trial on LT to solve a pressing difficulty.

A resplendent L90 (7711) photographed at Watford Tip during the early part of 1957. The oval brass plate on the leading splasher shows that 7711 had been built by Kerr Stuart, one of the many '57XX' panniers built by outside contractors. One feature of the panniers built by this contractor was the rivetted tanks thus making the first L90 and L99 easily recognisable. Note also that since being photographed when still 7711 (opposite) there has been an alteration to the pipework connected with the trip cock which is fitted behind the leading step and its red-painted actuating lever can be seen hanging below. This was to facilitate the fitting of an isolation valve.   *Colour Rail*

7711 is seen whilst on trials during the summer of 1956 at Watford Tip. That it was given an overhaul prior to coming to London Transport is shown by the sparkling BR black livery being carried. 7711 went on to become the first L90. It has already been fitted with trip cocks, probably of GWR pattern, during its overhaul but an isolating valve had yet be added.
Colour Rail

CHAPTER THREE
THE PANNIERS WITH LONDON TRANSPORT

The Western Region '57XX' pannier tanks are first mentioned in London Transport records in a memorandum from A. W. Manser to R. A. Smeddle, Chief Mechanical Engineer of the Western Region, at Swindon Works, dated the 2nd January 1956, in which Manser enquired whether trials could be carried out to ascertain if members of the '57XX' class would be a suitable replacement for the ex-Metropolitan locomotives.

In a letter from H. E. A. White, Motive Power Superintendent, Western Region of British Railways, to J. G. Bruce, Assistant Mechanical Engineer Running of the London Transport Executive at Acton Works, it is stated that a transfer of '57XX' number 7711 was being arranged, via Old Oak Common locomotive depot, to the London Transport steam shed at Lillie Bridge. Part of this arrangement was that 7711 would receive a heavy repair at Swindon Works before dispatch.

7711 arrived at Lillie Bridge Depot on Monday the 27th February. During initial trials carried out between Finchley Road and Baker Street the clearance above the outer edge of the cab roof caused some concern as the gap between the rain gutter and the bricks of the tunnel wall was only $2^{1}/_{4}$ inches. By relocating the rain gutter on the locomotive's roof it was hoped to improve this situation to give a clearance of 3 inches. The normal ruling clearance for this section was 4 inches.

An internal report, dated the 1st March 1956, listed the modifications that would be needed to make 7711 operable on London Transport including those to the cab roof rain gutters and the fitting of trip cocks as per all other London Transport locomotives. The document also asked what type of lubricating oil was used on Western Region locomotives and if any spare

water gauge glasses could be obtained.

On a further trial trip on the 8th March 1956, with Mr Percy Silverlock from the running department in attendance, 7711 was sent from Lillie Bridge to Neasden returning via Baker Street. Some modification to the rain guttering had been carried out and Silverlock wrote 'attended run last night 8th March 1956, four lead strips $2^{1}/_{2}$ inches long attached to widest part of cab roof, two each side on eastbound run. District Railway, Earls Court platforms, angle iron supporting footwalk just $2^{1}/_{2}$ inches clear of cab. In the tunnels between Cromwell Curve and High Street Kensington on north side clearance just $2^{1}/_{2}$ inches. But we think this is dirt not brickwork in the tunnel. On return run from Neasden 100ft approximately south of Swiss Cottage platform the clearance from the cab was $1^{1}/_{4}$ inches'.

A further test run took place over the same route the following night to try to improve the clearance on the locomotive's cab and rain guttering. Further modifications had been made to the angle iron strips on the cab roof which improved matters somewhat. A memo, dated the 15th March 1956, noted that the locomotive was at Lillie Bridge working in the yard pending general release and movement to Neasden.

London Transport must have felt that things were going well as a memo, dated 26th March 1956, from B. L. P. Cobb in the LT Purchasing Department was sent to the Western Region of British Railways, requesting lubricating oil and spares for 7711. Further test runs were arranged for the 24th and 25th April with Inspector Edwards of the Operating Department on a trip to Watford on 24th and to Aylesbury on the following day. A further trial to Aylesbury was arranged a few days later with a train of

MB

H. E. A. WHITE, M.I.Mech.E.
Assistant Power Superintendent

J. KERRY, M.I.Mech.E.
Assistant Motive Power Superintendent

Telephone
SWINDON 3611
Ext. 2403

Telegraphic Address
POWER RAILWAY SWINDON

BRITISH TRANSPORT COMMISSION

B.R. 32601/28

BRITISH RAILWAYS

MOTIVE POWER SUPERINTENDENT
WESTERN REGION
SWINDON, WILTS.

Our Reference 4328:33/9

Your Reference L.12/

Tuesday, 14th February, 1956

J.G. Bruce, Esq.,
Assistant Mechanical Engineer (Running)
London Transport Executive,
Acton Works,
Bollo Lane,
ACTON, W.3.

Dear Sir,

698544

       Exchange of Engines between Regions
       Boiler Replacement Programme -
         Steam Locomotives.

_____

       With reference to your letter of the 10th
instant, I am arranging to transfer to you shortly, Engine
No. 7711 which is now undergoing a "Heavy" repair in Swindon
Factory. It is anticipated that this engine will be released
on Thursday next, 16th instant, and the trip cock gear will
have been fitted whilst the engine has been under repair.

       I will advise you as soon as the engine is
ready for despatch to my Old Oak Common Depot and then for
forwarding to your Lillie Bridge Loco. Shed as mentioned in
your letter of the 13th January.

       Yours truly,

FOR H. E. A. WHITE

698267
60.07

The letter to J. G. Bruce relating to the arrival of 7711 on London Transport metals.

Transport for London Group Archives, LT254/1828

OFFICE OF THE		TO
DEPOT ENGINEER, EALING COMMON.		MR. L.R. COTTON, DIVISIONAL DEPOT ENGINEER 'A', ACTON.

OUR REFERENCE	YOUR REFERENCE		
PRS/IB	L.12/	DATE	29th February, 1956.

CHIEF MECHANICAL ENGINEER'S OFFICE.

1 MAR 1956

SERIAL NO. 700264   FILE NO.

EXCHANGE OF ENGINES BETWEEN REGIONS
BOILER REPLACEMENT PROGRAMME
STEAM LOCOMOTIVES.

With reference to the attached letter from the Assistant Mechanical Engineer (Running) to the Motive Power Superintendent, Western Region, Swindon, I would advise you that 'C' type Western Region Locomotive No:7711 arrived at Lillie Bridge Depot mid-day on Monday, 27th February.

I have inspected the locomotive and in my view it appears to be in excellent condition. There were, however, one or two points which I would bring to your notice.

(1)   The locomotive is fitted with tripcocks. These are mounted in the same position on each side of the locomotive, namely 8' 8" from the headstock and 19' from the tail stock. There are, however, no isolating cocks and in the event of wrong line working the trip arms would have to be removed.

(2)   I have checked the general outline of the locomotive to the drawings which you sent to me, and which are returned herewith, and find that the grab rails, hand rails and other protrusions, are all inside the gauge line. The cab roof, however, is not quite as shown on the gauge drawing and you will find a small sketch in the bottom right hand corner which shows that the maximum width is 8' $4\frac{3}{8}$" with a height of 11' $1\frac{1}{2}$" above rail level, due to pieces of angle iron attached to the roof so that we have, in effect, an increase of 3/8" over the dimension shown.

It would not be difficult to remove this angle iron which is riveted on one side of the locomotive and bolted on the other.

(3)   We should be glad to know the type of lubricating oil which is used by the Western Region in the mechanical lubricators.

(4)   The water gauge column glasses are not the same as our standard and I should be glad if you could obtain six of these glasses, together with the sealing washers, from the Western Region before the locomotive goes on its gauging run.

I have put in motion with the Rolling Stock Office for arrangements to be made for a gauging run and will advise you as soon as I have a definite date, in the meantime the locomotive is going to be steamed and worked in Lillie Bridge Yard so that the drivers can become familiar with its operation.

(1)—X
....um, 5/47—Stock)

Percy Silverlock's report on 7711 after arrival at Lillie Bridge.

Transport for London Group Archives, LT254/1828

The first L90 (7711) at Neasden shed during the winter of 1957, resplendent in London Transport livery but still sporting its BR smokebox door number brackets and vacuum and steam heat pipes. The driver's side trip cock can be seen fitted behind the leading steps.
K. Robertson collection

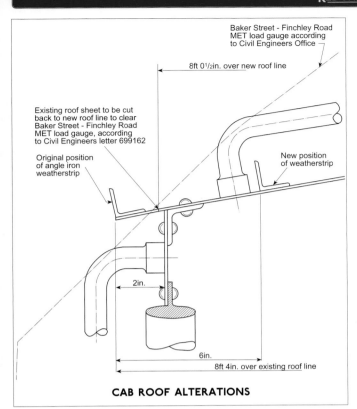

Baker Street - Finchley Road MET load gauge according to Civil Engineers Office

8ft 0½in. over new roof line

Existing roof sheet to be cut back to new roof line to clear Baker Street - Finchley Road MET load gauge, according to Civil Engineers letter 699162

Original position of angle iron weatherstrip

New position of weatherstrip

2in.

6in.

8ft 4in. over existing roof line

CAB ROOF ALTERATIONS

TRIP COCK OPERATION

The trip cock is a very simple but effective safety device fitted to London Underground trains and locomotives. It works by having a lever attached to a valve in the brake pipe of the train or locomotive. At the same level on the ground there is an automatic 'train stop' which is fitted adjacent to a signal. When the signal is red this bar rises up so that, should a train pass the red signal, the lever on the train or locomotive strikes this and the brakes are applied.

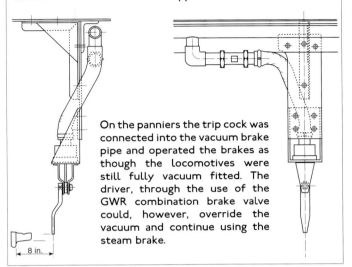

On the panniers the trip cock was connected into the vacuum brake pipe and operated the brakes as though the locomotives were still fully vacuum fitted. The driver, through the use of the GWR combination brake valve could, however, override the vacuum and continue using the steam brake.

8 in.

L90 (7711) while shunting the top sidings at Neasden, looking down on the storage yard full of 'COP' stock, then used on the Hammersmith, Circle and Uxbridge services, 13th April 1957. The position of the trip cock on the fireman's side can be seen between the centre and rear driving wheels piped directly into the main brake pipe. The actual trip cock lever hangs below just above rail height. *F. W. Goudie/Transport Treasury*

loaded flat wagons weighing 247 tons with a single brake van. At Aylesbury a train of loaded hoppers weighing 185 tons with two brake vans was taken on.

Inspector Edwards reported that the panniers had good visibility and steaming qualities. They also had no problem in maintaining boiler pressure or in maintaining scheduled timings. The report went on to state that from the braking point of view horse power was maintained when the brake was used as a steam brake rather than a steam and vacuum brake. There were problems with the trip cock apparatus when running slowly in reverse, the trip lever having lifted before the arm on the locomotive had gone by. Inspector Edwards also pointed out that after being tripped the driver of the locomotive could also release his brakes and proceed without setting the trip arm again. He added that there was no facility to isolate the trip cock.

There was a further memo on the 27th April from L. R. Cotton referring to the problem with the trip cocks whilst running in reverse, pointing out the need to solve this situation. On the 7th May 1956 the boiler of 7711 was examined at Neasden by the BR Western Region boiler inspector from Old Oak Common locomotive shed. There were no adverse comments on the condition of the boiler following this inspection.

A further memorandum, dated the 10th May 1956 to A. F. Collins stated that after satisfactory trials it had been decided by London Transport to use this type of locomotive as the standard type on all engineering trains. This would follow modifications to cab profiles and the fitting of trip cocks. These locomotives also had their lamp brackets changed from the GWR pattern to the standard pattern as used on other regions. In a further memo to Cotton on the 15th May 1956 reference was made again to the effective use of the steam brake over the vacuum brake while working on LT lines.

On the 20th November 1956 a reference was made to the comparative costs of overhauling steam locomotives at Lillie Bridge and Swindon. The latter were estimating at that time that they would continue to overhaul steam locomotives until 1967. The cost of an overhaul at Lillie Bridge was given as £2,500 as opposed to £1,500 at Swindon and this was the major factor in the decision that major overhauls would be contracted out. In the event Swindon ceased overhauling steam locomotives in 1965 and any further heavy overhauls would be carried out at Eastleigh on the Southern Region.

It was on the 19th November 1956 that arrangements were made for the purchase of 7711 and the transfer of the locomotive to London Transport stock. The book value, according to the Western Region, was £3,160 which London Transport found favourable. It was also decided to purchase a second '57XX', number 5752, the idea being to replace the ex-District and Metropolitan locomotives with ex-GWR panniers at the rate of one a year over the following five to six years. In fact the last examples, L89 (5775) and L99 (7715) were purchased in 1963 – exactly 100 years after Great Western engines first worked on the Metropolitan Railway in its opening year!

The decision to contract out heavy overhauls came at a time when it was becoming increasingly hard to recruit skilled workers for maintenance work at Lillie Bridge and Neasden. A memorandum of the same date, 19th November, refers to the problems met with in recruiting boiler makers and notes that there is only one employed at Lillie Bridge. On the same date it was decided to carry out the modifications to 7711 as well as repainting it in London Transport livery and allocating it the number L90.

Correspondence between L. R. Cotton and J. G. Bruce on the 19th February 1957 refers to the transfer of 5752 to London Transport, this locomotive becoming L91. The locomotive was modified and repainted in LT livery, and was ready to enter traffic in April.

On the 6th May the running department engineer informed LT management that ex-Metropolitan Railway 'F' class 0-6-2T number L49 had been withdrawn. Built by the Yorkshire Engine Company in 1901 it was originally Metropolitan Railway No. 90 and was replaced by L91 (5752). In addition 'F' class number

An immaculate L90 (7711) stands at Neasden on the 1st June 1957. The wooden cooling tower for the power station is a feature which appears in many views taken at this location and made an easily identifiable landmark.

R. C. Riley

Photographed at the same location was 'F' class 0-6-2 L49 which was replaced by pannier L91. L49, originally Metropolitan number 90, was scrapped in September 1957.
Lens of Sutton Association

L91 (5752) in the top sidings at Neasden on the 1st June 1957 only a month or so after its introduction to traffic and still fitted with its vacuum and steam heat pipes. Indeed it would seem that the first L90 and first L91 retained these throughout their short life with London Transport. 1938 stock, 'T' stock, 'COP' stock and 'F' stock can be seen in the yard below with the power station beyond.
R. C. Riley

An almost broadside view of L91 (5752) in the top sidings on the same occasion as the shot on the previous page, posed in a similar fashion to the view of L90 seen earlier in the volume. The locomotives were also fitted with curtains in the cab, presumably used to keep the worst of the fumes out whilst working in the tunnels. How effective these would have been is uncertain. It is also clear that the insides of the cabs were finished in black at this early period. However, later they were to be finished in the same turquoise (cerulean?) blue as the cab interiors of District stock albeit none of the colour views reproduced here confirm this .

R. C. Riley

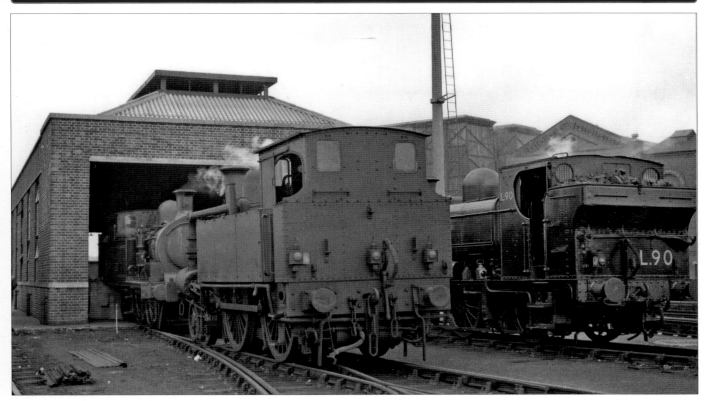

Three generations of Underground steam. The newly arrived L90 (7711) in company with 'A' class 4-4-0 tank Metropolitan number 23 (L45) and an 'F' class 0-6-2 tank in the 1930s built locomotive shed at Neasden c1957. *Hugh Davies*

Two of a different kind. Newly delivered pannier tank L91, 5752, the first to carry this number, and 'E' class L44, ex-Metropolitan number 1, at Neasden shed on the 13th April 1957. L44 would be later preserved, unlike L91 which was replaced in 1960 by 5757 which became the new L91. *F. W. Goudie/Transport Treasury*

L91 (5752) and 'E' Class 0-4-4 L46, both looking resplendent, stand outside the Neasden steam shed on the 1st June 1957. L46 was to have a few more years of life being scrapped in 1962. That there was a difference in the red paintwork is clear here with L46 being finished in more of a maroon shade – the old Metropolitan locomotive red. The panniers were later to carry a much browner shade of red. It is difficult to be precise on the colour and, as can be seen from images herein, there was much variation of the recorded image due to the differing emulsions of slide film types available in the 1960s and 70s.
R. C. Riley

An unusual view of the first L91 (5752) taken from an office block above Farringdon station late in 1958 showing the locomotive coupled to an ex-Metropolitan brake van on a works train.
F. H. F. Stacey

L51, Metropolitan Railway number 92, also built by the Yorkshire Engine Company in 1901, had been withdrawn in 1957 being replaced by L90 (7711).

A memo to L. R. Cotton of the 8th May refers to the shopping dates for the first two panniers, namely January 1958 for L91 and February 1960 for L90. However, in their early time with London Transport difficulties were encountered. There were problems with the brakes on L91 which meant that it could only be used for shunting until the problem was rectified. L90 did not experience any problems at this time as it was performing well but a further reference to L91 is mentioned by J. G. Bruce in that he suggested that they should dispense with L91's auxiliary reservoir and thus ensure that it was standardised with L90 which had already been modified. This involved leaving the pipe and vacuum gauge in position and a bleed hole being made in the reservoir, which was blanked off. In a letter from Smeddle the book value of the pannier was estimated to be £2,667 but L90 was transferred to London Transport for £1,485 which allowed for accumulated depreciation.

The condition of the ex-Metropolitan locomotives was getting worse and in a memorandum dated the 29th September 1958 reference is made to the disposal of L50 which had been withdrawn from service on the 21st March 1958. Again this was a 1901 product of the Yorkshire Engine Company having had the Metropolitan Railway number 91. In recent years these engines had been suffering increasing boiler and firebox defects. They had given good service over many years and had proved good value for money considering that they had been replaced in passenger and goods work after the First World War with much newer types that had, by the late 1940s, in LNER and early British

Railways service been withdrawn. On that basis both the 'E' class 0-4-4Ts and the 'F' class 0-6-2Ts had not only returned to passenger and goods service twenty years after being relegated to secondary duties but also survived on that work for fifteen years after withdrawal of their younger replacements. Few classes of locomotive in British railway history could claim such a record.

On the 29th December 1958 L90 had its boiler examined at Neasden by the Western Region boiler inspector from Old Oak Common who found it to be in good condition. In the meantime the problems with the older Metropolitan locomotives continued to plague LT with the Operating Department Engineer asking for panniers to replace 'E' Class 0-4-4T locomotives numbers L44 and L48 and 'F' class 0-6-2T number L52. This was on the 10th November 1959 and yet it was to take a further four years to totally replace the older engines.

The replacement programme for the remaining ex-Metropolitan locomotives continued as planned with pannier L92 (GWR 5786) being delivered in 1958, closely followed by L93 (7779) later in the same year. L94 (7752) was also delivered and was to become the locomotive which worked the last official steam hauled LT train on the 6th June 1971.

In 1960 the first L91 (5752) was sent to Swindon for boiler and firebox repairs and during the course of this work it was discovered that the work involved would be extensive and very costly. It was therefore found to be cheaper to offer London Transport a recently withdrawn pannier tank and hence 5757 became the new L91 in the place of 5752, this locomotive was originally to be numbered L96. Remarkably, a similar outcome resulted when L90 was sent to Swindon Works in 1961. For almost identical reasons the original L90 (7711) was replaced by

'F' class L50 (Metropolitan 91) on Neasden shed in the early 1950s. These locomotives were fitted with Westinghouse brakes around 1950, the brake pump being attached to the front of the tank and the reservoir on the tank top. By 1955 the fittings were giving problems on L50 as mentioned in the memo on page 20. Also apparent here is a curtain to shut off the cab opening and an oil can outside the cab side sheet in an identical position to one on L49.

Lens of Sutton Association

L91 (5752) at Swindon Works, probably late in 1960, having been sent for an overhaul it was failed on boiler grounds. It would seem that the ashes of the last fire have just been thrown out of the cab and that fittings such as the trip cocks have already been removed. Interestingly it still carries its vacuum and steam heat pipes showing that these were not removed whilst with London Transport.
R. A. Simpson, courtesy Colin Judge

Soon L91 was to be moved onto the dump at Swindon where it stood with other withdrawn locomotives prior to being cut up. It certainly looks rather less well cared for than in its early days with London Transport.   *J. Davenport/Initial Photos*

After being condemned L91 made its way to South Wales where it is seen en route to Morriston where it was to meet the cutting torch. Note the locomotive still has its connecting rods on – does this mean that the locomotive arrived under its own steam? Later when locomotives were regularly heading to South Wales for scrapping the rods were removed and the locomotives towed down. It is also still fitted with vacuum and steam heat pipes showing that these were not removed during its time with LT.   *Martin Davies*

Peckett 0-6-0ST L53, scrapped in August 1960, is seen here out on goods duties soon to be taken over by the pannier tanks. *Lens of Sutton Association*

7760 which became the new L90 on return to Lillie Bridge. Also in 1961, 5764 was delivered, being numbered L95, and this was followed by 7741, which became L96, a few weeks later.

The only other ex-Metropolitan locomotives withdrawn during the period of the pannier tank arrivals were the Peckett 0-6-0STs, L53 (Metropolitan 101) scrapped August 1960, followed by class mate L54 which was withdrawn during 1961 and scrapped in March 1962 at Neasden.

The scrapping of both the Pecketts left only one 'F' class, L52, 'E' class members L44, L46 and L48 and the District Railway Hunslet tanks L30 and L31. Within the next two years this would change further with the total extinction of all classes of steam locomotives with the exception of the ex-GWR pannier tanks.

In 1962 London Transport acquired a further two pannier tanks from the Western Region of BR, 7749, which became L97 and 7739 which became L98. In 1963, the Metropolitan Railway centenary year, the last panniers were delivered, these being 7715 which became L99 and 5775 which was numbered L89. Including the two replaced examples of the class London Transport had, since 1956, when 7711 was first tested, taken delivery of thirteen locomotives of the '57XX' class, even though in reality only eleven had been retained as part of the LT fleet.

However, there were those within London Transport management who, as early as April 1963, had concerns over the future of the panniers. A report compiled by the CME's office at Acton Works stated that the department had long term doubts over the continuing availability of overhaul facilities at Swindon Works for the panniers and that Western Region could only offer repair and overhaul services until 1967 at the latest. This situation posed a problem as the decision to purchase the panniers was partly based on the ability of Swindon to carry out these overhauls. As early as 1963 there were preparations in hand to replace the panniers with newly built battery locomotives or secondhand ex-British Railways diesel locomotives. In the event this situation would simmer on until 1969 when the

final decision to replace what was left of the steam fleet with secondhand Sentinel 0-6-0 diesels was finally made.

However, back in 1963 ideas were being outlined of using the battery locomotives that would eventually be cascaded from the Victoria Line construction project, or the purchase of secondhand BR 350 horsepower 0-6-0 diesel shunters. In the event the diesels were found to be unsuitable for the rapid movement of engineers' trains on the passenger carrying lines of London Transport. A secondary factor that did not help at that time was that, as with the J52 0-6-0 saddle tank in 1955, British Railways once more offered locomotives in a very poor condition, often fit only for scrapping. Again London Transport was less than impressed. Authority was sought for expenditure of £304,000 to cover the possibility of ordering thirteen battery locomotives to replace the panniers between 1963 and 1970 when it was envisaged that the last member of the class would be withdrawn.

At a CME's department meeting on the 16th June 1964 it was again stated that there was a need to plan ahead with a view to replacing the panniers with more modern motive power, especially as there would be no heavy overhaul facilities on British Railways for steam locomotives after 1968. At the time of the report there were eight battery locomotives available for use on the Victoria Line construction trains. However, after completion of these works only two would be required on the Victoria Line, leaving six as possible replacements for the panniers on general engineers' trains. It was noted at the meeting that, should this decision be taken, the locomotives should be replaced on a 'one for one' basis or by 'topping and tailing' trains with battery locomotives. It was also pointed out that there could be savings in staff if the latter practice was adopted as there was no need for firemen or ballast guards and their brake vans. However, in 1964 there were only four battery locomotives fitted with multiple control available.

Mr J. G. Bruce brought up the question of using battery locomotives for shunting at depots, mentioning that there were problems relating to visibility from the cab and also risk of damage to the locomotive's batteries. It was again felt that the purchase of a 350 horsepower shunter could be the answer for shunting within depots. In a letter dated the 21st July 1964 Bruce outlined the complex problem that London Transport faced in finding a reliable replacement for steam traction on engineers' trains.

Test runs were taking place through the summer months of 1964 of 'top and tailed' trains using battery locomotives. The trains thus did not require uncoupling or running around and they could be operated using just one motorman. The trials through the summer months of 1964 revealed that there were still problems with the reliability and suitability of battery locomotives on these trains. Although there was a degree of success in the trials it was still found that steam traction was more reliable and economic considering the hours worked.

1964 saw the scrapping of the last Metropolitan and District railway survivors. 'E' class L46 was withdrawn late in 1962 leaving five locomotives which were all taken out of service in July 1964. These were the two District 0-6-0s L30 and L31, 'E' class 0-4-4s L44 and L48 and the sole remaining 'F' class L52. Fortunately L44 was sold to the London Railway Preservation Society and is now based at Quainton Road. L48 and L52 were unlucky in that they were withdrawn before railway preservation had really taken off. At the time of the Metropolitan Railway centenary celebrations in 1963, L52 was an exhibit at Neasden and was officially photographed with Metropolitan Ashbury carriage stock which was on loan from the Bluebell Railway in

Sussex. It was hoped to preserve 'F' class L52 as an example of more modern Metropolitan motive power in the London Transport collection of historic rolling stock but, alas, as a result of a cracked main frame it was cut up for scrap.

At a meeting held on 14th August 1964 between representatives of British Railways and the London Transport Board there was a detailed discussion of the future of the steam fleet and the supply of spare parts. Mr P. R. Silvelock of the running department opened the meeting by outlining the current situation and pointing out that LT intended to retain the panniers until 1970. BR stated that they were willing to overhaul L94 and also L95 which was in poor condition, needing extensive boiler repairs and work on the cylinders. It was agreed that BR Western Region would retain two spare reconditioned boilers and a quantity of spare parts with a view to future heavy overhauls. Reference was also made to stored '57XX' panniers at BR Western Region sheds that could be sold to London Transport as replacements for any locomotives that were in need of heavy repairs. The cost of heavy overhauls, beyond the facilities at Neasden and Lillie Bridge, was now £3,200 per locomotive against some £1,300 for a good secondhand replacement pannier. The arrangements for the heavy overhauls carried out by BR Western Region would guarantee a further 80,000 miles of service for each locomotive. BR also pointed out that ancillary services, such as wheel, tyre and brake cylinder replacement, should still be available to LT in the future.

At a further meeting on the 18th August 1964, held at 55 Broadway, the issue of replacing the steam fleet with battery

L99 stands close to the coaling stage at Neasden with the power station in the background. This was brought into use in 1904 in connection with the electrification of Metropolitan services.
Mike Morant

On the 14th July 1969 L89 is seen at Neasden on train working 510 as denoted by the drop in numbers in a frame attached to the bunker, a similar frame being attached to the smokebox door. It would seem that these were fitted at some point around 1968 with the numbers referring to the specific working of the train. The polished black finish of these locos at this period was due to improper cleaning. At Neasden an old oil drum full of a 'patent' mix, possibly oil, paraffin and a silicone wax, was kept stirred and this was applied by the cleaners. The problem was that the dirt was not cleaned off first and so became covered by the mix. The silicone set and so at the next cleaning was polished and the dirt was encapsulated! Apparently it took a wire brush to then get back to the red. The same applied to the buffer planks which really were bright red. *P. Watson*

locomotives was once again raised. Worries were now raised about the future of staff at Lillie Bridge and Neasden if steam was withdrawn as the drivers and firemen were not trained on the battery locomotives. There was also concern over the use of battery locomotives on engineers' trains between Amersham and Aylesbury without auxiliary power from conductor rails. The question was discussed further on the 30th September 1964 when the need for good reliable shunting locomotives to replace steam was raised. With the doubts about the suitability of using battery locomotives for prolonged periods of shunting at depots it was suggested at this meeting that a new type of electric steeple cab locomotive might be the solution to the problem. Costing for such a locomotive was discussed against the cost of a battery locomotive and it was found that even a small locomotive of this type would prove too expensive.

The matter of overhauls and heavy repairs also came to the surface again as British Railways Western Region had been contacted with a view to the use of the facilities at Swindon Works and they had replied that they would not be available after the end of 1966. This would effectively seal the fate for any locomotive requiring serious work after this date. However, it was suggested that none of the locomotives would require this before 1968.

It was pointed out at another meeting, held on the 20th November 1964, that in order to provide a battery locomotive to carry out all the shunting and ballast train workings of a steam locomotive it would need to be on charge for eight hours before each period of use; both shunting during the day and ballast working in the night. Further to this situation at a meeting held on the 22nd March 1965 it was pointed out that no matter how they viewed this situation it would still require two battery locomotives to do the work of one pannier tank and that the existing battery locomotives had severe limitations over the long hours required on engineering trains and the shunting

associated with such duties. To emphasise this point a copy of a graph curve, No. 505D, was provided in a report of the 29th March 1965 which clearly showed that the pannier tanks were more suitable for this type of work. It had already been confirmed that no British Railways diesel shunter could travel at even 30mph when required, unlike the pannier tanks which achieved higher speeds in order not to interfere with the normal service trains.

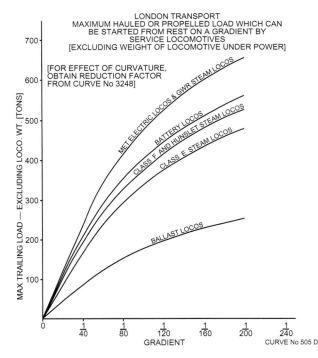

At a meeting held at Acton Works on the 18th March 1966 chaired by Mr J. G. Bruce it was pointed out that the last heavy overhaul of a pannier tank had been carried out at Eastleigh Works on the Southern Region of British Railways and that from now on any locomotive requiring a heavy overhaul would have to be withdrawn for scrap. A table was drawn up which allowed for four to be withdrawn at the end of 1967 and a further two by the end of 1968, another two by the end of 1969 and the last three by the end of 1970. This would be the end of all eleven pannier tanks on London Transport. Mr Bruce went on to state that if necessary he would allow locomotives to be withdrawn before the dates on the draft plan which would allow for any untoward incidents such as a collision or major defect to a locomotive without interfering with the need for a set number of locomotives for regular use.

Any question of London Transport being able to return to carrying out heavy overhauls at Lillie Bridge was discounted as this was felt to be no longer an option. One solution considered to the use of battery locomotives was the construction of them with removable battery boxes so that these could be charged while the locomotives were in use. Another possibility was the hiring of BR diesel shunting locomotives for use at Lillie Bridge and Neasden yards and whether testing could take place. Tests with a 350 HP diesel shunter took place soon after this meeting with staff from Neasden receiving training at Harlesden Yard on the London Midland Region but after half a dozen men had been trained nothing further developed from this initiative. It is probable that the management at the time were considering purchasing more battery locomotives or diesels of their own built to London Transport specifications.

During 1966 L96 (7741) was withdrawn, the first pannier since 1961 to be removed from the fleet. The second, L91 (5757), followed in 1967 together with L93 (7779) in the same year. In 1968 the withdrawals continued with L97 (7749) and L98 (7739) being taken from the fleet.

At a meeting on 21st May 1968 chaired by Mr H. T. Steele it was stated by Percy Silverlock that at present there were seven steam locomotives, although one was possibly due for withdrawal later in the year. A new table was drawn up suggesting that two locomotives be withdrawn in 1969, one in January and one in July, with two further withdrawals in January 1970 leaving two retained for a short period for shunting in Lillie Bridge and Neasden – the last of the remaining six available for service. A training programme was also set up for steam staff and ballast guards to prepare them for the new arrangements when steam was finally replaced.

During 1969 the withdrawals of panniers continued with L92 (5786). By good fortune it was purchased by the Worcester Locomotive Preservation Society and moved to the Bulmers Cider factory at Hereford being the first of the surviving panniers to be preserved. Fortunately this trend continued with all the remaining panniers being purchased for preservation.

In a report dated the 29th April 1970, compiled by the C.M.E. Railways office, the question of the development of a battery locomotive for shunting was again raised with reference to a report compiled following a conference held in October 1968 when this concept was again discussed in relation to the replacement of the steam fleet. The idea of hiring a British Railways diesel locomotive and crew had, by this time, been ruled out. The need to design such a battery locomotive was discussed at great length with cost being a major factor. It was estimated that a suitable locomotive would cost in the region of £50,000 including development costs. The main reason why it was felt that existing battery locomotives could not perform the same tasks that the pannier tanks carried out was that the visibility from the tube gauge locomotives was severely

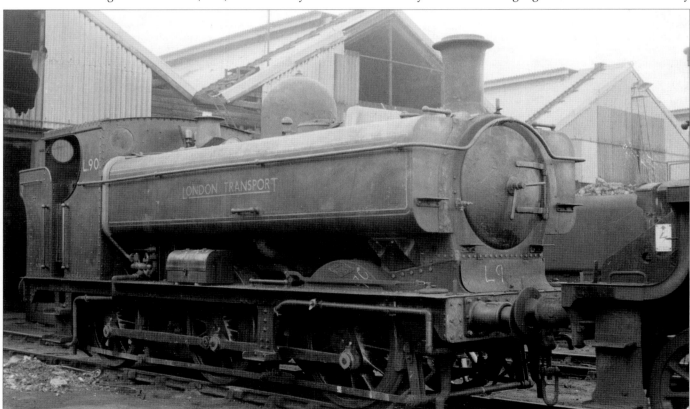

L90 (7760) at Eastleigh shed c1965. This was the last overhaul carried out by BR for London Transport. The work was carried out in exchange for the loan of a rail welding machine for use on the Bournemouth line electrification completed in 1967. It would seem that for working over British Railway lines the trip cock gear valves and levers have been removed

G. Wheeler

Another view of L90 on the Southern Region, possibly on its way back from Eastleigh Works 19th December 1965. It was captured at Basingstoke shed.
Keith Harwood

L98 was photographed in June 1965 at Lillie Bridge and reveals an interesting feature – a lagged pipe runs from the steam cock on the front of the smokebox down to the running plate and then back beyond the tool box. The purpose of this is unknown.
Keith Harwood

restricted. In addition there were still concerns over battery damage and damage to the controls during shunting.

At a meeting in September 1966, it had been hoped to retain a small number of panniers for shunting until at least 1971 or 1972. However, as a result of the lack of heavy overhaul facilities at British Railways' workshops, and a lack of spare parts, it was suggested that the replacement of the panniers should occur sooner rather than later. In particular there was concern over the general condition of L90 (7760), which had boiler and firebox problems. Of the remainder L95 (5765) was in the best condition and posed little concern in maintenance terms. L94 (7752) had some minor technical defects but it was felt that these could be rectified to retain the locomotive in service for the period required. It was also believed that maintenance facilities would become more deficient, especially at Lillie Bridge Depot. The possibility of one of the surviving locomotives not being available could cause serious embarrassment to the Chief Mechanical Engineer. It was also noted that the Chief Operating Officer was pressing for their early withdrawal due to maintenance difficulties.

The London Transport Executive had yet again investigated the possibility of purchasing 350 horse power diesel locomotives from British Railways but to no avail due to the poor condition of the examples on offer which had been robbed of parts. They once again considered hiring in locomotives of this type as and when required and a quote was obtained from British Railways and £5,800 per year was mentioned for each locomotive including maintenance.

It was felt that the replacement with electric locomotives might be an advantage but the cost of developing such a locomotive, together with the fact that due to the length of time before delivery, which would be after the last steam loco was withdrawn, would defeat the object of this exercise. The possibility of purchasing a diesel locomotive of a proven design was also investigated and

was found to be £30,000 per locomotive. British Railways offered three diesel hydraulic locomotives at £16,000 each and this was also considered. This price included a full service prior to delivery and the fitting of couplings suitable for use on London Transport rolling stock. Authority to purchase three locomotives at a total cost of £48,000 was sought as provision had been made in the capital expenditure budget of £90,000 for this purpose.

At another undated meeting in 1970 one finds the first reference to some secondhand diesel locomotives available from Thomas Hill, plant dealers of Rotherham. Three 0-6-0 Sentinel diesel hydraulic locomotives were offered at £48,000, fitted with Rolls Royce engines. Built in 1967 they had low mileage of around 20,000 miles. The decision to purchase these three Sentinel diesel shunters was only reached after exhaustive studies and the obtaining of tenders from other locomotive manufacturers and suppliers, such as Hunslet, English Electric, A.E.I. and Andrew Barclay who could not supply what was required or quoted prices beyond the allotted budget. Approval was sought to purchase the three locomotives from Thomas Hill to replace the remaining pannier tanks which it was estimated had a book value of £8,791. These became DL81, (built in 1968) delivered on 12/03/71, DL82 (1967) delivered on 25/05/71 and DL83 (1967) delivered 07/06/71.

During 1970 a further two panniers had been withdrawn and sold for preservation, these being L89 (5775) sold to the Keighley & Worth Valley Railway in Yorkshire and L99 (7715) which was sold to the London Railways Preservation Society at Quainton Road, Oxfordshire, now the Buckinghamshire Steam Centre.

In a draft report dated the 29th July 1970 it is stated that a price of £54,000 had been agreed for the three Sentinel diesel shunters, which included overhaul prior to delivery. Because of the short wheelbase of these locomotives, only 9ft 8ins, it was advised to fit a short four-wheeled tender in order to allow the locomotives

A fine study of L93 standing outside the steam shed at Neasden in June 1965. Close inspection of the front footstep reveals that a bracket has been added below the step itself. The purpose of this was unclear until the arrival of the two images opposite. The photograph also shows that the brackets for the train reporting numbers still have not been fitted at this date.

Keith Harwood

L92, in what must be the most photographed location at Neasden, shows a beam added on to the bracket beneath the front step. Locomotives known to have been fitted with this feature were L89, L90, L92, L93, L94, L95 and L99.
J. E. Connor

A close-up of the front step of L89 gives full detail of the wooden beam and shows it to have been for carrying sleet brushes complete with their screw down adjusters. One such beam would have been fitted either side to sweep the outside power rails clear during winter weather. A third bar was attached under the locomotive, believed to have been below the leading axle where in BR days the automatic train control (ATC) shoe would have been attached. The brushes on this could only be lowered when the locomotive was over a pit. The high axle weight of the panniers probably made them ideal for such work. To the right of the beam can be seen a handle connected to a bar which was used to reset the trip cock as access to this was made difficult by the beam.
Ron Head

to work over the track circuiting of the running lines. These were built using redundant bogies from scrapped 'Q' stock cars and resembled shunter's trucks.

The last three panniers soldiered on through 1970 and into the first months of 1971, showing all the expected signs of maintenance problems. L90 (7760) causing continued concern owing to the condition of its boiler and firebox. L94 (7752) was judged to be in good condition having had a heavy repair at Ealing Common Depot and having had its wheels dropped out of its frames to cure excessive sideplay in the horn blocks. Its boiler and firebox were in good condition. L95 (5764) was in the best overall condition in spite of a loose tyre on the driving wheels which had been welded.

The condition of all three locomotives was covered in a brief report dated the 12th March 1971, probably produced with a view to the sale of the panniers and by now there were many interested purchasing groups. A date was set for the end of steam on London Transport, Sunday the 6th June 1971, after which the three green painted Sentinel diesels would take over shunting duties from the panniers. This marked the end of an era, not only for London Transport but for the nationalised railway system as a whole as the panniers were the final standard gauge steam locomotives in service in Britain on a public railway. London Transport would give its last steam locomotives a wonderful and emotional send off, just like that which had been provided for the trams in 1952.

Right: L89 is seen at Watford after taking water whilst on the Neasden to Watford Tip working. The train was taken as far as Watford where it reversed to return to the tip.
Geoff Plumb

Only a week from withdrawal L90 was captured at speed near the signal box at Neasden from a passing train whilst working light. A week later, on the 6th June 1971, such workings would become history.
A. Smith

L95 marshalling an engineers' train in the yard at Neasden in December 1969 amongst 'A60' Stock.

Ron Head

L89 at Ealing Common Depot on the daily stores train working from Lillie Bridge which also took in Northfields Depot and Acton Works. Materials typically carried were coal for the forges at Acton Works and new tyres and brake blocks for the passenger stock whilst taken away was material such as swarf from the wheel lathes going for scrap.

Ron Head

Kirk and Laddi, fellow cleaners at Neasden in the spring of 1968.

Kirk Martin

CHAPTER FOUR
WORKING WITH THE PANNIERS
KIRK MARTIN

In 1968, while working as a second man on diesels at Stratford Depot, East London, I found myself missing the atmosphere of steam I had known when I started work on the railways in Derbyshire. I decided to find out whether London Transport was still using the steam engines I had seen when I had been at school in West London before my parents moved to the Midlands.

I made my way to Lillie Bridge Depot, close by West Kensington station, and there they were – two ex-Great Western pannier tank engines simmering on shed while a third was shunting the extensive permanent way yard. I spoke to the inspector in charge and he advised me to go to Griffith House near Edgware Road station. I went there on a later occasion and was given an interview and, after a couple of weeks, was offered a job as an engine cleaner.

I handed my notice in to British Railways and, kitted out with overalls from Acton Works, was sent to the Railway Training Centre at White City to learn my rules and regulations. I must have been the only person on that course heading for a steam shed as the others were trainee guards. I remember that the Railway Training Centre had a large model railway to explain signalling regulations. According to the London Transport Museum the whereabouts of this are now not known.

The vacancy for which I had been taken on was actually for Neasden, the other London Transport steam shed, and after passing my rules test, I made my way to Neasden station and entered the Metropolitan depot walking up the long roadway past the massive car sheds full of the silver Met 'A60' stock trains. At the far end of this there were extensive sidings leading from the north end of the shed to my right and the Metropolitan and the Bakerloo lines to my left. There, tucked between the two, was the small two road steam shed open at both ends so that you could see right through it. At the far end there was a coal stage on the right and ash pits on both roads. A water column stood between the two roads and there was a pannier tank alongside the coal stage.

I signed on and met the staff on shed including two other young cleaners, Joe and Laddi. Having been given a locker and shown where the mess room was I joined them out in the yard. Here I was back to cleaning engines again and I was soon busy rubbing down warm metalwork as trains rattled past on the running lines. Those pannier tank engines, in their maroon livery, were kept clean in comparison to the steam engines I had known at Derby that were within a couple of years of coming to the end of their working lives.

In the spring of 1968 charge driver Harry Robinson positions a coal wagon alongside the coal stage at Neasden shed. Note the London Transport owned 16-ton mineral wagon whose number unfortunately cannot be seen. It was obviously acquired secondhand from British Railways as the position where the number and other details would have been carried on a black-painted patch can still be seen.   *Kirk Martin*

Driver Richard Cox oils up a pannier tank at Neasden, 1968.

Kirk Martin

As well as cleaning engines the charge drivers, like Harry Robinson (now in his eighties and still a friend) would set myself, Laddi and Joe to work at shovelling out the ash pits, cleaning the mess room and sawing sleepers for fire lighting. Occasionally we were told to run errands to offices at Baker Street and Griffith House. This was a chance to leave the steam shed and travel on a Bakerloo line train to Baker Street or Edgware Road to drop and pick up packages. Back at Neasden I sometimes went over to the power station canteen for lunch and once explored the insides of this impressive building going up and down a network of metal steps and walkways.

Back on shed one of the hardest jobs we had to do was unloading coal from a 16-ton wagon onto the coal stage. One of the panniers would position the wagon alongside the stage and two of us would climb up onto the coal. Unloading the wagon was hard work at Neasden because the stage was too high for us to drop the side door of the wagon and we therefore had to start digging down from the top of the coal. This was exhausting work and it only got easier when we reached the wagon floor where you could at last slide the shovel along under the coal. Once there, of course, you still had the high side of the wagon to heave the coal over.

In the mess room senior drivers, like Harry Robinson and Richard Cox, an ex-Metropolitan Railway man, would smile at us new lads and tell us about the old days working on the old 'E' class 0-4-4T and 'F' class 0-6-2T engines on the Ricky to Aylesbury passenger trains and local goods turns. Harry Robinson had even fired the last of the 'A' class, 4-4-0 tank engine Number 23, built to haul passenger trains on the Metropolitan Railway lines through London. However, going back outside to heave coal and shovel ash in 1968 didn't seem so different to me.

Right: Armison poses alongside a pannier tank at Neasden shed – summer 1968. *Kirk Martin*

Coal flies through the air as Armison and Joe heave coal out of a 16-ton mineral wagon onto the coal stage at Neasden. *Kirk Martin*

Cleaners duties. Taken from inside Neasden shed three panniers are seen around the water column with the coaling stage on the right whilst Joe waters the ash pit to keep the dust down. Joe is also seen below undoubtedly thinking of days, or nights, out on the main line away from Neasden once passed out as a fireman. *Kirk Martin*

Driver Harry Varley at Neasden shed on L98 during the summer of 1968. He had joined London Transport in 1947 after three years firing on the Southern Railway. *Kirk Martin*

Shedmaster George Freshwater, driver Richard Cox and foreman Raymond Woods at Neasden. Richard Cox had started his working life on the Metropolitan and by 1968 was approaching fifty years service. *Kirk Martin*

After a few months it was my turn to pass out for firing duties on the engines. I was to join the crew on the daytime Watford Tip train, which took rubbish wagons out to the tip alongside the Grand Union Canal near Watford. I would be firing the engine under the supervision of the fireman and driver. Having already had a go at firing steam engines, during my time on the railways in Derbyshire, I was looking forward to the experience.

I signed on for my first trip on L92 (5786) on the 23rd June 1968, joining the driver and fireman in preparing the locomotive and then running over to the yard by Neasden Power Station to pick up our train. It was good to be layering fresh coal around the bright firebox and opening the warm water and steam valves of the injectors on this, the first trip of the week. Getting the right away from the guard the driver swung the reverser lever over and tugged at the regulator.

Running bunker first, as was usual heading north, my driver eased the train out of the yard and we were soon dipping down through the fly-under and heading out through Wembley Park and along the Met Main Line through Harrow on the Hill, Pinner and Northwood. I swung the flap down and put a few shovels of coal around the firebox as directed by the fireman and got the hang of working the injectors, opening the water and steam valves and then tapping the water valve slightly until the overflow pipe reduced to a trickle as we rocked along.

We took the junction round to Watford, passing through Croxley Green station and crossing the Grand Union Canal to run into Watford Metropolitan station where we left our train on one of several sidings adjacent to the platform. We took water at the water column on the platform, which meant climbing up onto the

L89 works up the gradient from the underpass out of Neasden Depot and is approaching Wembley Park station with the works train to Watford Tip, as a southbound Bakerloo line train of 1938 stock heads for Baker Street (no Jubilee Line then!). The tracks in the foreground are the BR lines from Marylebone. June 1969.   *Geoff Plumb*

L91 heads south through Pinner with the returning empty spoil train from Watford Tip to Neasden Depot on a cold but sunny Monday 13th February 1967. The headshunts from Pinner Goods Yard were still in situ but disused by this time.   *Geoff Plumb*

A driver's view from the footplate of L90 waiting for the road into Harrow on the Hill on the Metropolitan Main Line in January 1970. The signal has just changed from red to yellow so the train will soon be on the move. To the right of the running rails just past the gantry can be seen the position of the trip cock device – the signal having changed the bar has gone down.
Ron Head

tanks and manhandling the 'bag' into the tank. We re-coupled to our train, which had a guards van at each end, and clanked back through Croxley Green and the cutting to Watford Tip, alongside the canal between Lot Mead and Common Moor locks. Shunting our wagons, grinding up and down the sagging tracks to position the loaded ones and pick up empties, it was eventually time to make up our train and start rolling back to Neasden.

As we clattered along the Met Main, between the bright silver service trains, it was exhilarating to feel the breeze on your face and look across to the driver, standing on his side of the cab, observing the line ahead. The fireman told me to start burning the fire down on the way and we were soon rolling slowly through Wembley Park station and switching into Neasden Yard. A bit of shunting and then it was onto the loco shed to dispose of the engine, have a wash and get off home.

Over the next few days I fired L90 (7760) on the same trip and I finally took my firing test with Inspector George Freshwater on board L94 (7752) at the end of the week. On this trip the injectors started playing up and at one point Mr Freshwater had to work the valves. He stood, nodding to me as the water in the overflow pipe reduced to the perfect trickle and the pipes began to sing, indicating that the injector had picked up and was sending water into the boiler.

Because of this I was dreading the news at the end of the trip that I had failed but he called me into his office later on in the day and congratulated me in having passed out, I was now a passed cleaner (known as a 'passed fireman' in LT terminology just as what I knew as a 'passed fireman' was called a 'passed driver' on LT). It was back to cleaning engines and sawing up firewood again but being available to act as fireman when required in the

yard or on the night time engineers' trains. However, before one of these turns came my way I applied for, and was lucky enough to get, a transfer to Lillie Bridge, where I had already been sent on a couple of occasions when they were short of cleaners. An advantage was that it was closer to my home in South London.

Although there was some overlap, Lillie Bridge provided engineers' trains for the District Line as Neasden did for the Metropolitan. There was a large yard with engineering materials, sleepers, rails, and a huge 'Goliath' crane spanning the sidings. Like Neasden, Lillie Bridge was staffed with fitters and several loco crews to cover duties in the yard and on engineers' trains. It is remarkable to me that both Neasden and Lillie Bridge were operating in 1968 in very much the same way that Harry Robinson had described to me when he started back in 1940.

I was on cleaning duties again – but it wasn't long before I got my first turn. This was on the 'yard engine'. My driver was a large West Indian called Johnson who said little but had a great chuckle which made his belly shake. We shunted up and down the yard – often disappearing under an overhead structure near Lillie Bridge Road where our steam and smoke would ripple under the concrete beams to be drawn out as we came surging back out into daylight. Our job was to assemble the trains for the late evening departures.

I was a bit over cautious at first and Mr Johnson had to nod at the fire and point up at the steam pressure gauge at one point as the engine became sluggish – a few quick rounds on the fire and the shunting regained some vitality. This was very useful experience for what was to follow. This was my first run on a service train on one of the daytime trips to Ealing Common Works and a full description follows on page 53.

A pannier and brake van set off from Lillie Bridge down towards Kensington Olympia where it will run back into the BR sidings on the far side of the West London Line to pick up wagons containing materials for LT. The West London Lines are on the right and the LT line to West Kensington passes under the bridge below the brake van. Note also the 1927 standard stock motor end now converted to a ballast motor. *Kirk Martin*

The view in the opposite direction off the Cromwell Road bridge shows the two lines curving off to the right which gave access to West Kensington station on the District Line to Ealing Broadway / Richmond. The District Line itself can be seen at the lower level heading under the bridge to Earl's Court station. The lines off to the left give access from the depot down towards the West London Line and Kensington Olympia. The steam shed is on the extreme right and just discernible alongside it is Peckett L54, therefore dating the view as pre 1961. *Lens of Sutton Association*

An unidentified pannier (possibly L97) shunts the BR sidings alongside the West London Line. The line up into Lillie Bridge Depot is on the extreme right. The depot itself is beyond the Cromwell Road overbridge. Stood alongside the train is a rake of Southern Region horse boxes.   *Colour Rail*

A very tidy L89 is seen at Kensington Olympia on a materials train off British Railways for London Transport at Lillie Bridge.   *P. Fink*

SUNDAY 18TH AUGUST 1968

I arrived at Lillie Bridge to sign on at 07.00 for a general cleaning and shed duties turn. Driver Johnson and fireman St Leonce on yard loco. Driver Dick has turned up for the Ealing trip. The driver who is acting inspector today said the fireman for this train had not signed on yet so I said 'I'll keep my fingers crossed' and he looked at me with surprise saying that if I was passed out I might as well get on the engine straight away.

My driver Dick moved the loco, L90, onto No. 2 road and I climbed up on the tanks to fill them. This is my first running turn as my first firing turn was shunting in the yard. At 08.00 the fireman turned up, over one hour late – my heart sank. The acting inspector came over and said that he had opted to stay on shed and I was to stay on the engine – it was possible that he would get a chance to knock off early once his shed work was completed.

My driver said not to build the fire up too much as we only had a light load on – a few wagons loaded with rails and a brake van at each end. We left Lillie Bridge Yard with the boiler full and 180lbs on the steam pressure gauge. We lurched down the tight bend into West Kensington station and rolled through Barons Court. The steam pressure began to fall back at Hammersmith, where people stood back as we clattered through the platforms. As I suspected, the centre of the fire was very thin – it was a bit too light for the load after all. Generally, I found, the panniers liked a thicker fire around the edges and thinner in the centre but not so that you could see the bars!

By now we were storming up the line towards Ravenscourt Park and I fired to the back corners and placed several shovels of coal over the centre and front corners. I closed the fire doors and fully opened the damper. The steam pressure was creeping up as we passed through Stamford Brook so I reached down to open the injector to fill the boiler with water but Dick advised me, with a shake of the head, 'not to just yet'. I leaned out as we were slowing down through Turnham Green. We got the signal and Dick opened the regulator up and we started pounding along with the reverser lever thumping in its frame.

We passed through Chiswick Park with the injector now singing and then slowed right down at Acton. The signal came off as we were rolling towards it. It felt good to lean from the cab as Dick opened her up and we stormed through the platforms. There is a climb to take you over the bridge at the junction and we now had sufficient steam and water to top the summit. As we came to a rest in the platform at Ealing Common – with an interested audience looking on – I wiped my forehead with a cloth to complete the show.

We got the signal and propelled the wagons back into the yard. The steam level was coming round as we ran to the far end and dropped down the bank and then ran back into a siding at the back of the sheds and gangers unloaded the rails while we dropped down slowly. After this we had a lunch break. It's good to have your tea and sandwiches sitting on a pile of sleepers while the engine is simmering quietly alongside you. The guard produced some plums, which he had got from a laden branch overhanging the sidings. After a while I started to make the fire up so that we had nearly the full pressure by the time we started shunting the yard prior to running back to Lillie Bridge Depot.

Two lads were looking on as we backed down into Ealing Common station and I closed the fire doors and fully opened the damper. The signal on the platform end cleared and we were off. I put the injector on as we rattled through Acton Town. As we rumbled over a long viaduct I saw a woman and child looking up from a road below – they waved and I waved back. Later on I was sitting on the small folding seat as we were approaching

L95 approaches Acton Town on the 15th May 1970.

Gordon Wells

An unidentified pannier at Stamford Brook station with a train of BR steel and 5-plank wooden open wagons. It is probably returning from Acton Works after the delivery of finished parts or heavy duty wire in the autumn of 1969. This train is on its way to Lillie Bridge from where the wagons will eventually be trip worked across to the BR sidings via Kensington Olympia.   *J. Haydon*

Three panniers, including L95 on the left, stand on Lillie Bridge shed between turns.   *photographer unknown*

Chiswick Park and I saw a cloud of steam in the distance and we were soon passing another steam loco, a light engine bound for Neasden.

Round through Turnham Green I closed the injector and watched out for signals. Passing Stamford Brook a girl turned as her boyfriend pointed at us. We rattled through Ravenscourt Park and down the bank into Hammersmith and slowed down through Barons Court. At West Kensington the dolly was off at the end of the platform and Dick opened the regulator wide to send us lurching and grinding up the twisting track that climbed up to cross the running lines and take us into the yard at Lillie Bridge.

After shunting our wagons we ran onto the shed. I cleaned the fire and shovelled ash out of the smokebox while Dick refilled the bunker from the coaling stage. Then we had a good wash and had a mug of tea in the mess room before booking off.

After this it was back to cleaning duties again. There were also the ash pits to empty and the coal wagon to unload. This was easier at Lillie Bridge because the coal stage, made of concrete rather than of wood as at Neasden, was low enough for the side door of the wagon to be dropped down. As soon as it was dropped a load of coal poured out onto the stage. As with

Neasden this was a two person job, but here one of us would shovel coal out of the wagon and the other shovel it further into the bunkers at the back of the stage.

Another duty we cleaners had was cleaning the mess room where there was a radio always on. As well as listening to the latest pop music I remember hearing the news of the Soviet Union's invasion of Czechoslovakia while mopping the floor and wiping the tables in that mess room. We also kept the panniers reasonably clean – clambering over the tanks with a good supply of cleaning rags. Later on I had a few 'preparation and disposal' turns with drivers Harry Capel and Chris Green, assisting the crews with coaling up and cleaning fires and smokeboxes.

I was lucky that several turns came my way, when I was booked on as a cleaner on nights, which enabled me to gain some more experience with the pannier tank engines. These were on ballast trains out to the east of London towards Barking and Upminster.

A detailed log one of these trips is given on page 62.

The driver assists at the end of the day by coaling up, heaving the coal from the stage into the bunker while I take a break from clearing the ash pan and smokebox to take a photograph – Lillie Bridge summer 1968.
Kirk Martin

SHUNTING AT LILLIE BRIDGE

Taken towards the end of 1968 an unidentified pannier is seen shunting alongside the stores building in Lillie Bridge Yard. One end of the Goliath crane which straddled the yard can be seen. A plan of the yard appears on page 112

Kirk Martin

On the same occasion the train passes the photographer and heads off down the yard. In the background stands the Empress State Building, completed in 1961 to a design for the Admiralty and intended to look like the bow of a ship from any angle. *Kirk Martin*

L92 shunting Lillie Bridge Yard comes round the corner of the Signal Shop, the northern end of the long building divided into workshops and stores. Buildings along the Cromwell Road can be seen in the background. *Kevin McCormack*

L95 shunts at the southern end of Lillie Bridge Yard on the 16th March 1967. In the background can be seen the stockpile of stores used for renewals on all parts of the underground system. Here were kept sleepers (both new and reusable) crossing timbers, bridge timbers, chairs and rail lengths, all sorted by size and length and accessible by the Goliath overhead crane which would load the rail flats and sleeper wagons. The Goliath could be run the entire length of the yard and one of its rails can be seen crossing the siding immediately in front of L95. Details of the various engineering wagons used can be found in Appendix Two.   *R. K. Blencowe*

L95 is seen at virtually the same point on the 17th July 1970 by which time it had gained the train reporting number brackets on the smokebox door. The photographer was taking advantage of a break from work whilst attending an exhibition at Earls Court having discovered that steam locomotives could be found at work during the mornings just outside when all other main line steam had finished.   *G. Moon*

Although taken on a slightly murky winter morning with evidence of recent rainfall this view of L95, taken on the 12th January 1971, is included as it shows a range of the road vehicles used by London Transport to move stores and equipment around. The lorry in front of the pannier is fitted with an hydraulic crane immediately behind the cab. The long building in the background housed various sections of the works and stores departments including the signal shop, a machine shop and a saw mills.   *G. Moon*

L90's safety valves are just lifting whilst shunting on the 4th March 1971. Coupled next to the engine is flat wagon number F381. Notice that one of the flap over buffers is in the raised position. Apparently it was fairly common to shunt with one buffer raised – it certainly made access easier for the shunter himself. The buffers were made to hinge over so that when the Underground pattern Ward coupler was in use they were not in the way. Notice also that the sleet brushes are fitted under the leading footstep.

G. Moon

On the 25th July 1970 L94 is about to pass under the concrete beams carrying an extension to a car park which was built over the southern end of the yard. It was here that Kirk remembers often disappearing under whilst shunting the yard. Today this area has undergone further redevelopment with the building of the extension to the Earls Court Exhibition Centre. *G. Moon*

The fireman and shunter discuss the next move whilst L95 stands in the sunlight on the 23rd July 1970. The trip cock must be isolated as the lever is in the up position, facing towards the front of the loco, probably as shunting is taken place the driver is only using the steam brake. *G. Moon*

On the far side of the sleeper stacks two roads ran parallel with the old electric car shed. L95 is seen shunting with two of the Ashford-built brake vans, some flat wagons and three ballast hoppers at the rear on the 18th July 1970. *G. Moon*

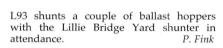

L93 shunts a couple of ballast hoppers with the Lillie Bridge Yard shunter in attendance. *P. Fink*

After passing the camera the shunter stands with his pole at the ready to uncouple and cut the hoppers to make up a train. *P. Fink*

With the shunter riding on the cab steps L97 shunts in Lillie Bridge Yard. *Kirk Martin*

Fireman Samuels at Lillie Bridge shed. *Kirk Martin*

Lillie Bridge loco inspector Joe Lowe with footplatemen Tom Power and Pat Bourke. Joe Lowe had begun his career with the Metropolitan Railway back in the 1920s and by 1968 was in charge of the three panniers at Lillie Bridge.
London Transport Magazine, July 1968

SUNDAY 8TH SEPTEMBER 1968

I booked on at 22.00 and prepared L98 for driver Ken Green and we hooked up to the stock at the wrong end – this enabled us to propel the wagons, with a brake van at each end, down into West Kensington station. Getting the signal we then stormed off through the tunnels, with the steam swirling around the cab pierced by the glare from the fire, to emerge into the cutting near Earl's Court where my driver slapped the cab sides and shouted to some gangers on the track 'the old girl made it'. They laughed and shouted back that they had been 'taking bets on it'.

We ran through the platforms at Earl's Court and out through the tunnels via Victoria, St James's Park and Tower Hill. It is interesting that in the tunnels at night there is a strange reversal of the usual in that stations are in darkness and deserted while the tunnels are often lit by tunnel lighting and Tilley lamps and were alive with gangers attending to the track – I had to take care how I used the injectors when passing them due to the scalding steam that could burn them. After pausing at Whitechapel, to speak to the gangers, we were soon on the open-air section of the old London Tilbury & Southend Railway local lines passing through Barking and Elm Park on route to Upminster.

We came to a stand at a signal on the approach to the vast Upminster Depot – the engine simmering quietly in the cold night air. Suddenly a voice crackled out from the vicinity of the signal. To my surprise my driver called out our train details and these were picked up by a microphone and relayed to the signalman who threw the switch to give us a green light – there was something incongruous about that high tech world and the steam engine we were on. We took water and ran around our train and had some tea and snap before heading back on the westbound line.

We stopped with our train on a section of line near Plaistow while the gangers unloaded rails and materials and got to work. I tried to keep the engine quiet while we stood for some time. It was good to sit chatting in the cab between the warmth of the fire and the cold of the night air while the scrape of shovels and clatter of materials reminded us of the work going on outside.

Eventually I built the fire up and we were on our way again with the steam pressure rising as we headed back towards Lillie Bridge. We got stopped at Gloucester Road by a red signal and I sat on the platform bench for about twenty minutes before Ken called to me as we had a green light. We had taken longer than expected on our homeward run and we rolled back through Earl's Court station as early morning passengers were standing on the platform waiting for the first District Line service – they stepped back as we came clanking through with our brake vans and work stained wagons – the sound of the rods echoing around the cavernous station.

At West Kensington we stopped before getting the signal to propel our train back. Ken set back with the long train and brake van approaching the points at an increasing speed. The train lurched and the flanges squealed as we pounded back up the twisting track to Lillie Bridge Yard. There we left our train for the yard engine to sort out and we ran on to the shed to dispose of our loco – this means cleaning the fire, ash pan and smokebox and topping up the tanks and bunker before knocking off and cycling home at 06.30.

As well as engineers' trains to Barking, Plaistow and Whitechapel we would occasionally take wagons of rubbish or materials over to Neasden. These trains involved running out along the Piccadilly Line to Rayners Lane where we ran round before heading down the Metropolitan Main Line to Neasden. On one trip we went over with L90 and returned with L95, a useful way of transferring locomotives from one shed to the other.

L94 working train 551 just west of Upminster on the District Line engaged on picking up worn rails in April 1970. Notice the temporary lighting rigged to give some illumination on the work in hand.
Gordon Wells

L95 on train working 500 ready to depart Barking in December 1969. *Gordon Wells*

In the real black of the night L94 had stopped to unload its train to the east of Elm Park by the use of Tilley lamps only. April 1970. *Gordon Wells*

L94 with train 551 paused on its return to Lillie Bridge in the platform at Tower Hill station. *Gordon Wells*

Later on I had two consecutive nights on this turn using L94 from Lillie Bridge to Neasden and back, the first with driver Chris Green and the second with driver Harry Capel. I recall leaning out of L94's cab at Sudbury Town and looking back down the train at the brake vans on either end of three flat wagons and the steam billowing back over the rails and curling away as a large fluffy cloud catching the glare from the street lamps on an adjacent road.

At Neasden there was time to have a mug of tea and eat our snap in the mess room before preparing our engine and running down though the tunnel passing under the Metropolitan tracks and out through Wembley Park to Rayners Lane on the Uxbridge Branch where we once more ran round our train and headed back to Lillie Bridge in the early dawn. We would occasionally pass the Ealing Common train at Chiswick Park or Turnham Green creating the amazing sight of two steam hauled trains passing each other in London in 1968.

At Lillie Bridge we also went over to the sidings on the far side of the British Railways West London Lines – running down towards Olympia to gain access to these sidings. Here we would pick up and drop off wagons with supplies for our permanent way yard and loco department. Between moves we would sit in the warm cab of our little pannier tank loco watching the diesel hauled BR trains rumble past. These trains were the same that I had been working on not so long before when I was based at Stratford Depot on the Eastern Region. By this time steam was well and truly finished on BR and we must have been the last non-preserved steam locos to travel over BR lines.

As well as firing on the pannier tanks I had an 'awayday' on steam of a different kind on the 20th August 1968 when I volunteered for a mid-week turn on the Bluebell Railway in Sussex. Here I fired the little locomotive *Bluebell* to driver Jack Owen on several trips between Sheffield and Horsted Keynes. I remember finding the pannier tanks much more powerful than the little South Eastern & Chatham 'P' class when I booked on at Lillie Bridge the following day.

Generally, the crews at Neasden and Lillie Bridge were very satisfied with the panniers. As Harry Robinson said, they were 'right for the job', although he did admit that with their little GWR wooden flap seats for the driver and fireman they were not as comfortable to work on as the old Metropolitan locomotives. I suppose the GWR did not expect their crews to spend much time sitting down on the job – and in fact neither did we. The LT drivers stood there, caps pulled well down, and sent those panniers rattling along. Keep layering the fire, keep an eye on the water and steam and they were happy.

I returned to Neasden shed on one occasion and arrived just as some contractors were cutting up one of the stored panniers alongside the shed. I had my camera with me and took some photographs of the butchered remains of one of these sturdy and hard working engines. Fortunately six of the others were later to find homes on several of our preserved railways and can be seen today – sometimes running in London Transport livery. I returned to Lillie Bridge knowing that the days were surely numbered for the panniers.

Sadly, I made the decision to leave London Transport in order to return to college to belatedly take my GCE 'O' and 'A' levels. I handed my notice in and as I walked away from the shed on my last day I thought that I would never step onto the footplate of a steam engine again. In fact, twenty years later, I joined the loco department of the Bluebell Railway and became, once again, a steam fireman working on a wide variety of locomotives. Looking back I am very glad that I made the decision to move over to LT in 1968 and also that I took my camera to work with me to record this oasis of steam.

Although Lillie Bridge shed has been converted into an office suite, Neasden retains some of its steam age atmosphere as it has hosted the engines used on the very popular 'Steam on the Met' events. Sadly this worthwhile venture which gave a great deal of pleasure to staff, the public and local schools, as well as raising money for charity, is not operating at present. The ash pits and coal stage at the north end of the shed have gone but a glimpse of a steam engine outside the shed a few years ago brought the memories flooding back.

A driver's eye view of Neasden steam shed from L90, May 1971. *Ron Head*

Driver Christopher Green of Lillie Bridge shed oiling round before working an engineering train in 1968. The photograph was used as part of a feature in *London Transport Magazine*, LT's house journal, on the panniers and the fact that they would become the last steam locomotives in general use. Christopher Green was born in Barbados and in 1968 had been working on LT for thirteen years of which six had been as a driver out of Lillie Bridge.

London Transport Magazine

THE PANNIERS AT WORK

L94 at North Harrow returning to Neasden with empties on the 7th June 1960.

A. Delicata

L97 on a train mainly composed of mineral wagons passing Acton Town, eastbound, circa 1965.

Colour Rail

L95 heads the breakdown train, including the ex-Metropolitan steam crane, back to Neasden in the summer of 1962. This was during a period of improvements on the Metropolitan Main Line between Moor Park and Northwood where a severe traffic bottleneck was being resolved by quadrupling the track and bridge replacements. Note the lettering on the tanks is in a higher position. *photographer unknown*

L90 (2) in later London Transport red livery at Neasden with a permanent way riding van number B.554. This vehicle had been built in 1914 by the Metropolitan Railway as a ballast brake van on a secondhand underframe. It was scrapped in November 1969. *Colour Rail*

Two and a half years after the Western Region had done away with steam traction on the 2nd January 1966 a red pannier, L95, sneaks out through Paddington station in the dead of night – the platform clock showing 01.20 in the morning, on Saturday the 24th May 1969 thereby cocking a snook at the BR steam ban and raising the banner for former GWR steam in London. L95 is seen whilst standing at Platform 15 on an engineers' train heading for Hammersmith Metropolitan.

Frank Dumbleton

On Thursday the 8th September 1966 L94 was caught near Pinner Green trundling along the up fast line on a short train of empty ballast wagons heading back to Neasden.
Geoff Plumb

L92 with a 6-plank wagon PH94x – a wagon dedicated to servicing the power station at Neasden and here loaded with ash from the boiler grates.
Keith Harwood

L99 passing through Earl's Court station light engine in the late 1960s.

Ron Head

L94 with a short train consisting of a BR all steel wagon and a Hurst, Nelson brake van via Kensington Olympia station. This was a regular daytime working.
Dr Ian C. Allan/Transport Treasury

L90 propels its engineer's train out of 'the hole' at Farringdon after being engaged in re-sleepering work on the widened lines.
Ron Head

After running round its train L90 passes through Farringdon station on its way back to Lillie Bridge. *Ron Head*

At the western end of the station L90 crosses over to regain the Circle Line. *Ron Head*

WATFORD TIP WORKINGS

Over the next few pages a trip will be taking with the Watford Tip working from Neasden to the tip at Croxley. Whilst always a regular working the intensity increased in the late 1960s with the demolition of the power station at Neasden and the consequent disposal of material. L89 is seen above preparing the train in Neasden Yard while L90 stands alongside in the summer of 1968.

Kirk Martin

L93 approaching Northwick Park station running on the Up fast Metropolitan Line track with the return empty wagons of the spoil train heading back to Neasden Depot. The tracks in the foreground are the former Great Central Railway route into London Marylebone station. Note on this occasion that the two brake vans are marshalled at the rear, normally there would be one at either end. April 1967.

Geoff Plumb

L98 makes a furtive dash through Harrow on the Hill in the summer of 1968.
D. Knapman

A guard's eye view of a returning empty spoil train approaching Harrow on the Hill.
Ron Head

The same train as seen above running into Harrow on the Hill station. *Ron Head*

L93 approaching Pinner Green, April 1967. *Geoff Plumb*

L97 bowls along the down slow line at Pinner Green, May 1967. Brake van B.564 was a 10-ton ballast brake built in 1894. *Geoff Plumb*

L95 trundles through Pinner station as it returns from the tip at Croxley with empty wagons for Neasden Depot. The spoil train ran from Neasden to Croxley ran every day Monday to Friday and was especially busy during the demolition of power station at Neasden. July 1969.   *Geoff Plumb*

On a wet day in the summer of 1968 an unidentified pannier speeds a train of empty bogie open wagons through Northwood on its way back to Neasden from a working to Watford Tip.

J. E. Conner

L89 works bunker first as always through Croxley station en route for Watford. There it ran round its train and took water before returning through Croxley to the tip just by Watford South Junction. June 1967.

Geoff Plumb

L95 passing through Croxley station heading to Watford before retracing its steps. July 1969.

Geoff Plumb

On a sunny but freezing cold day in January 1969, L94 approaches Croxley station from Watford, where it has run-round its works train from Neasden and is now heading for the tip at Croxley. Note the steam crane in the consist of the train.   *Geoff Plumb*

A murky wet morning sees an unidentified pannier passing through Croxley with the tip working.   *J. E. Connor*

L89 taking water from the tower at the end of the platform at Watford station whilst running round its works train from Neasden before returning to the tip at Croxley. September 1969. The water tower was later dismantled and re-erected at the Buckinghamshire Railway Centre, Quainton Road.

Geoff Plumb

These two images explain the pattern of clean patches on the tanks of L89! The engine is being watered at Watford station, rather over-enthusiastically, the water cascading down the sides and cleaning as it goes! The engine has arrived with the spoil train from Neasden and has still to regain its train and take it into the tip at Croxley for unloading. September 1969.

Geoff Plumb

L92 brings a wagon full of burning rubbish to the water column at Watford to enable the flames to be doused. *Kevin McCormack*

Snow lies on the ground as driver Ray Woods swings the bag back round after filling the tanks of L90. His fireman balances on the handrail whilst attending to some matter in front of the cab.
Ron Head

L97 rounds the curve from the Watford direction at Watford South Junction and is about to enter the siding to the tip at Croxley with the spoil train, Monday the 31st October 1966.
Geoff Plumb

L89 enters the tip at Croxley passing a couple of decrepit looking steam cranes which seem to be out of use. September 1969. It is difficult to say which cranes were allocated to the tip but there were over a dozen three- to six-ton cranes on the books.
Geoff Plumb

L97 at Croxley Tip with a train of spoil wagons during shunting operations prior to returning to Neasden with a train of empty wagons. Monday 31st October 1966. L97 was one of the ex-GWR engines built by North British, its diamond shaped builder's plate still carried on the front splasher.
Geoff Plumb

L89 shunts on the tip near Croxley with the daily spoil train from Neasden Depot. Ash and other material was carried, some from Lillie Bridge which had been tripped round to Neasden. Note the steam cranes for unloading the wagons. June 1969.
Geoff Plumb

L95 shunting on the tip at Croxley, the shunter hitching a ride on the cab steps after the engine has uncoupled from its train. January 1969. *Geoff Plumb*

The fireman on L94 gives the fire some attention during shunting at Watford Tip. Note the reversing lever on the driver's side of the cab takes up much of the available space, but made for much quicker shunting moves than a screw reverser! May 1968. *Geoff Plumb*

The driver of L94 has one hand on the regulator and keeps a good look-out as the train is propelled out of the sidings at Watford Tip and onto the main running line from Watford at Watford South Junction, before reversing and heading back to Neasden Depot. *Geoff Plumb*

The crew of L94 offered to take Geoff all the way to Neasden on the footplate, but sadly he had to turn the offer down as his motorbike was at the tip at Croxley. Accordingly, he got down from the engine after it had propelled its train out of the tip and was deposited on the trackside adjacent to the third rail! L94 now sets off towards Neasden at Watford South Junction, the points for the tip (just visible on the other side of the bridge) having been reset. May 1968.

Geoff Plumb

L89 has propelled its works train out of Watford Tip sidings and onto the main line from Watford and is now setting off back to Neasden at Watford South Junction. The lines in the background are from Aylesbury and Amersham. September 1969. The return train was usually empty but this one has a load of logs in the first wagon!

Geoff Plumb

L97 having finished shunting at the tip near Croxley, propelled its empty wagons out onto the main line from Watford and then set off back towards Neasden at Watford South Junction, just passing the entrance track into the tip. Monday 31st October 1966.

Geoff Plumb

The view from the footplate of L94 at Watford Tip.
May 1968.
Geoff Plumb

L89 sits in the sunshine at Watford Tip, having just arrived with the spoil train from Neasden via reversal at Watford. After shunting the loaded wagons it then departed with empty wagons to return to Neasden Depot. June 1967.

Geoff Plumb

CHAPTER FIVE
FOLLOWING THE PANNIERS
THE PHOTOGRAPHERS

GEOFF PLUMB

I was born in Sheffield where I first discovered railways at a very early age due to the enthusiasm of my father, Derek. In 1957 we moved to London, living in Harrow Weald, not too far from the West Coast main line where I watched 'Princesses', 'Duchesses', 'Scots' and 'Jubilees' as well as some of the older LNWR 0-8-0s on freights.

Later we moved to the borders of Hatch End and Pinner when steam was obviously on the way out and it became a mad dash to photograph as much as possible before it disappeared. As I was still at school and the cost of colour film was relatively expensive I resorted to working three paper rounds and a Saturday job in a green grocer shop, which, although generating income, reduced the opportunity for photography.

By the time I started work in 1967 the only main line steam workings left were on the Southern Region and these finished in the summer. All that was left were a few pockets in the North West, industrial steam and, of course, London Transport. I took a few shots of the loco shed at Neasden Depot from passing trains, noting that it did not look the sort of place that could be entered unofficially, unlike some of the main line sheds!

I then discovered that spoil from the recent demolition of the power station was being taken to the tip alongside the Grand Union Canal near Croxley and that these trains were being hauled by the ex-GWR pannier tanks that I had seen on the shed. What is more, these trains were running in daylight hours. These now became a target for my camera between longer trips to Manchester, National Coal Board lines and South Wales.

Sometimes it was a case of nipping down the road to Pinner Green where a convenient footbridge crossed the line or to Pinner station, where none of the staff seemed troubled by a teenager with a camera. Because of the track layout the tip was only accessible from the southbound line from Watford and the trains, which had a brake van at each end, had to run all the way to Watford where the engine ran around its train and, after taking water, retraced its steps to Watford South Junction to gain access to the tip.

The train was shunted at the tip, the full wagons being left behind and the empties being returned to Neasden. Several steam cranes were used at the tip although I never saw them in action. The return train was propelled out onto the southbound line before running back to Neasden. It was quite easy to get to the tip – there was a small unsurfaced track which led from the main road into the middle of the triangular junction which was suitable for my motorbike and I went on several occasions to watch and photograph the shunting operations which could be quite complicated and took some time.

On one occasion a particularly friendly loco crew invited me to join them on the footplate whilst the remainder of the shunting

A second view of L89 sitting in the summer sunshine. June 1967.

Geoff Plumb

took place. I took some further shots from the cab and, when the shunting was completed, was invited to stay with them all the way back to Neasden. As my motorbike was parked in the tip, and I could see no apparent means of getting back there, I sadly had to decline the offer but I did ride out with them to the main line where I took a further photograph as they awaited the signal to proceed.

Main line steam having finished I was venturing abroad, making my first trip to Northern Ireland in September 1968 and on returning I joined London Weekend Television as a trainee cameraman – furthering my interest in photography. Travelling to the LWT studios in Wembley Park gave me further opportunities to photograph the panniers at work.

Apart from the operations at Neasden there was also Lillie Bridge Depot near Earls Court which I managed to see on only one occasion while hanging over the wall alongside the Great West Road near West Kensington. I also managed to photograph one of the panniers on a train near Ravenscourt Park.

By now, with an increased income, I had purchased a Pentax SLR camera and tried it out on the pannier workings to Watford. By 1970 this train was in the hands of battery locos, 'topping and tailing' the train so that no running round or brake vans were necessary although reversal at Watford was still needed. The panniers could still be found at Neasden although the Sentinel diesels were also seen on the shed.

All too soon the 6th June 1971 saw the final demise of the pannier tanks and London Transport ran the 'Last Steam Train on the Underground' to mark the occasion. It was all over. Thankfully I had my memories and photographs of the red panniers at work in their final years.

The shunter at Watford Tip hitches a ride on the cab steps of L97 as it runs round some wagons during shunting on Monday 31st October 1966.

Geoff Plumb

L94 shunting wagons on the tip at Croxley, May 1968, with brake van B.581, built in 1962 under contract by BR at Ashford. Six were acquired to replace some of the old Metropolitan vans and were numbered B.580-585. *Geoff Plumb*

The shunter rides on the cab steps of L95 at the tip in January 1969. The shunter's pole is resting on the buffers and coupling hook. The brake van on this working, B.559, was built by Hurst, Nelson in 1935 for the Metropolitan and it survived until 1984. *Geoff Plumb*

At Watford Tip in September 1969 L89 is seen shunting its wagons around to drop off the ones full of spoil and collect the empties to return to Neasden Depot. The brake van, B.582 was also built at Ashford in 1962. *Geoff Plumb*

L89 has dropped off the full wagons and now just has two brake vans behind the bunker, the train it will take back to Neasden Depot is on the left of the picture, unusually, one of the wagons is loaded with logs, perhaps there was a ready sale amongst depot staff. *Geoff Plumb*

With its cylinder cocks open, L89 has made up its train of an empty wagon and two brake vans and is now propelling them out of the tip at Croxley, before returning to Neasden. Note the supply of coal for the steam cranes in the nearest wagon. June 1969. *Geoff Plumb*

L89 with its cylinder cocks open approaches Watford South Junction after leaving the tip at Croxley to return to Neasden. June 1969. *Geoff Plumb*

L94 with a couple of ballast wagons at Lillie Bridge on the 15th March 1970. There would appear to be some relaying going on, possibly in connection with the extension of electrified lines within the depot. The original Piccadilly Line car shed, now in use by the Engineering Department, stands on the left whilst the steam shed is on the right.
Gordon Wells

GORDON WELLS

Being a fireman at Stratford shed in East London in the 1950s and 60s which had many cross London diagrams - working from Temple Mills to yards south of the River Thames - the route, via Kensington Olympia, passed Lillie Bridge Depot which meant that a glance over that way would reveal how many pannier tanks were on shed. There would usually be two visible in the late evening but on our return, after midnight, they would be out on their night's work. Steam working finished at Stratford in 1962 but I retained my interests in the job, becoming a driver on diesels in 1965.

Having been a member of a local model railway club for some years I had met there two other members who worked for London Transport at Upminster Depot. All three of us were shift workers so keeping in touch was intermittent. However, one of them handed me a copy of the *London Transport Magazine* for July 1968, which contained an article about the last of the pannier tanks still at work. The seed of an idea was sown – to take photographs of the engines at work at night.

Another year passed and, with only the trio of L90, L94 and L95 still remaining in service I took chance trips in my Land Rover in the hope of sighting one of these engines at work. I concentrated on the east of London, at Campbell Road, which is halfway up the steep 1 in 40 climb from Bow Road to Bromley by Bow. I also went to Salisbury Avenue, Barking where there was a water tank. A chance sighting of a pannier tank at Campbell Road was always satisfying. Another sighting while parked in Campbell Road about the usual time, between half past midnight and one in the morning, was not a steam engine but an urban fox on the prowl! More common now this was a rare sight in those days. Coming straight from work one night and parking in my usual spot in Salisbury Avenue I was questioned by two of Barking's bobbies on their beat. Recognising my railway uniform they were soon on their way.

It was not until the autumn of 1969, however, that one of my LT friends, working in the Control Tower at Upminster Depot, told me of a steam working which coincided with my shift pattern. Accompanying him to work at 22.00 in the Control Tower overlooking the extensive sidings time passed quickly talking shop, drinking tea and taking photographs within and without the tower.

The expected train arrived just after 02.00 hauled by L90. By the time L90 had run round its train and drawn up to take water I was positioned to take my first time exposure photographs. Water taken, and with my photographs exposed, I had a brief conversation with the driver. Although L90 sounded in good order, he did not consider her the best of the trio and it was usually stationed at Neasden rather than Lillie Bridge. He told me that the train would draw down by the mess room giving me another opportunity to take a photograph.

During our conversation uniformed figures emerged from the guards van next to the engine. They were two Metropolitan policemen taking the opportunity of having a ride behind a steam engine. Returning to the control tower to thank my friend I set off just after 03.00 to walk to Gidea Park station to catch a train home. It was some months later that I once again met the driver of L90 and learnt the tale behind the appearance of the policemen.

They had, apparently, been parked in their patrol car near Whitechapel station when they had heard the sounds of a steam engine and gone to the platform to investigate, managing to cadge a ride on the train to Upminster and back to Whitechapel where the driver left them with the parting shot 'I hope no one's nicked your car'. From these experiences it had become apparent to me that it paid to have friends on the inside and also that the wearing of railway livery gave one some diplomatic immunity!

News of only one steam working reached me in late December 1969 which I managed to photograph as usual by time exposure using my tripod. This train, hauled by L95, I then followed to

An overall view of the District line depot at Upminster with 'R' stock, 'Q' stock, and 'CO'/'CP' stock present.

Gordon Wells

The control panel within the tower at Upminster Depot showing line occupancy and allowing point operation using the black turn switches. The transistor radio was probably not part of the standard equipment!
Gordon Wells

L90 and its train is seen drawn up outside the mess room at Upminster. Being a timed exposure the zig-zag of light shows the passage of a member of staff with a Tilley lamp.
Gordon Wells

L90 taking on water at Upminster on the night of the 1st/2nd October 1969.

Gordon Wells

Upney but lost it passing Becontree. The photographic results, however, were encouraging in these unusual lighting conditions. Stratford drivers were still reporting sightings of the panniers when working goods trains over East London lines.

Having lost contact with my two LT friends by 1970 I visited the Train Crew Supervisor at Upminster and he was helpful. Yes, he assured me, there was a working on Saturday, and a very wet night it turned out to be. I had better luck when I approached the Station Inspector at Stratford station who was able to share with me the LT engineers' workings giving me more opportunities to follow any steam workings when my shift permitted.

Of more than a dozen trips, some being in daylight, only brief memories remain. Travelling by road at 03.00 one Sunday morning with a friend to Ealing Broadway we found the station locked. However, being in railway uniform gained us admittance and we were able to see and photograph L95 on an engineers' train. Another night trip by road to Acton Town, this time my friend, more an accomplice, was carrying a portable tape recorder, sadly the recordings have not survived. There were no opportunities for photographs this time but my accomplice was invited onto the footplate of L95 which was dropping ballast from hopper wagons.

On completion of this work my friend came over, grinning from ear to ear, and told me that he had been invited to join them on the trip back to Lillie Bridge leaving me to return by road. However, I was able to join them later on the trip at Barons Court station where I was to meet two people I was to come to know well over the next year or so, Driver Johnnie Harris, who I had met at Upminster, and passed fireman (or 'passed driver' as they called them on LT) Terry Coleman. The engine was of a class I had seen many times shunting at Acton when on one of Stratford's many cross London freights.

Being some years since I had been on the footplate of a steam engine at work I was very pleased when the driver invited me into the cab. The step up from the platform to the footplate gave me an immediate feeling of being at home. As the fire door was closed the only illumination came from the lamp on the water gauge which showed the area of the footplate swept down as it should be after firing had taken place. It was interesting to compare this ex-Great Western Railway engine with the ones I had been familiar with, such as the Great Eastern Railway 'Buckjumper' J69s 0-6-0 tanks or the N7 0-6-2 tanks which we had had at Stratford. Apart from the presence of the shin high coil springs on the panniers there was the boiler pressure of 200lbs which was higher than the 180lbs of the GER engines.

During our conversation the work continued. For some reason the ballast would not run from the hoppers and this necessitated us repeatedly pulling up the train and then stopping and setting back to shake up the ballast and, no doubt, the guard. Our conversation ended when the signal cleared for the run back to Lillie Bridge. This involved running to West Kensington and taking the sharp climb up to the yard where the train was disposed of and the engine screwed down on the coal stage.

L95 with train about to depart Upminster for the return trip to Lillie Bridge.

Gordon Wells

It was April before the opportunity presented itself to plan another trip. Travelling by road to Barking to catch the last service train to Whitechapel we found the Station Foreman waiting to lock up for the night. My explanation that I was waiting for a steam hauled engineers' train was accepted and, should it be cancelled, there was still time to get the night bus back to Barking. Well before the passage of the eastbound staff train, the muffled sound of a Great Western loco could be heard and a single lamp over the buffer was seen approaching round the curve of the platform. Coming to a stand there was some banter from my friend John about railway photography as he stepped down onto the platform. His fireman, Terry, shutting off the injector said 'had I known you were coming I could have stayed at home!' All this chatter brought several gangers out onto the veranda of the guards van to add their comments and while the photograph was being taken the Station Foreman came over having seen the last eastbound train away.

The signal cleared for us and, with only a light train, L90 climbed easily up the gradient from Bow Road to stop at Bromley by Bow where we ran around and crossed over to the westbound road to start the night's work, drawing forward to stop at the point where the London, Tilbury & Southend Railway line to Fenchurch Street diverged to pick up used materials. Remarkably a Class 31 BR diesel was engaged on similar work on the LT&SR lines. The driver was a colleague from Stratford well known for his interest in steam engines and he soon walked over to climb up into the cab of L90. A conversation relating to steam engines and engineers' trains was soon in full swing to be cut short by a ganger from our train telling us to move towards Whitechapel.

Stopping between Whitechapel and St Mary's Junction, where there is a branch leading down to the East London Line to New Cross and New Cross Gate, our team began to pick up worn rails by hand by the light of Tilley lamps and the tunnel lighting. The drawing down and stopping to pick up each 60ft length gave me ample time to leave the footplate and take some time exposure photographs.

Back on L90 again I got into conversation with John while Terry kept a look out for hand signals from the gangers. We talked about the working of trains in tunnels. Having been a fireman in the East London Gang at Stratford in 1957, working mainly goods trains but also some excursion passenger trains from Liverpool Street to New Cross, where they were bound on Southern Region metals, double headed with a pair of J69 'Buckjumpers', I was well aware of the problems of working through tunnels. Some of my drivers were very competent but some were very nervous of the claustrophobic conditions of the single bore Thames Tunnel.

John assured me that he had to stop down there many times to drop off or pick up rails. He then went on to describe the method he adopted when unloading the long 300ft sections of welded rail from a specially constructed train. The rail would be run off the rear wagon as the train drew slowly forward but the last few feet would spring up dangerously as they dropped. By counting the exhaust beats from the chimney a shrewd idea of the distance covered could be gained and he knew when to ease up to drop the end of the rails slowly.

During our conversation Terry had been keeping a look out for the gangers' hand signals telling John when to draw forward and stop for each rail to be loaded which was accompanied with much crashing and shrieking of steel on steel. We were by now standing in what remained of St Mary's station and John pointed out what was left of the platform and the wooden frame of the original signal box. With the last of the rails loaded we set off for Lillie Bridge Depot.

L95, working train 551, in December 1969 stops for water at Barking. *Gordon Wells*

Under the illumination of sodium lamps L95 is glimpsed standing at Upney station on the District Line in December 1969. *Gordon Wells*

L94 and crew at Upminster on the 1st May 1970. The driver on this occasion was John Harris.

Gordon Wells

Another chance sighting of a pannier occurred early one morning when working a return goods train from Willesden to Temple Mills in full daylight between Brondesbury and West Hampstead where the Metropolitan and Great Central Joint lines pass overhead. An engine and train was approaching on the embankment above, trailing a plume of white exhaust steam. A sight which brought to mind the line in Auden's poem 'Night Mail' that describes the train 'shovelling white steam over her shoulder' for that is exactly what this unidentified member of the trio was doing as she hurried her train towards Neasden.

In mid 1970 I was expecting one, if not all, the remaining engines to be taken out of service. I visited Lillie Bridge one afternoon with one of my LT friends as guide, both coming straight from work and in uniform. After contacting the man in charge and gaining permission we were able to photograph L94 and L95 on shed. He assured us that as far as he knew they would be at work for some months to come.

A week or so later I travelled to Lillie Bridge on the last westbound service for a trip to Ealing Broadway on L94 with Terry as driver, John being the night charge man. I was surprised at the enormous fire that had been put on L94 but, as it transpired, this lasted all night. There followed a straightforward trip to Ealing Broadway where we ran round the train and then stood for several hours giving me ample time for photography. With tight fitting dampers L94 wasted no steam from her safety valves and was ready for her return run as soon as the ganger gave the OK that his work was finished.

Another trip with Terry and L94 was out to Uxbridge. This trip was punctuated by running over a single detonator approaching Sudbury Hill. After stopping a look out man was seen walking towards us showing a red light. He allowed us to draw into the platform where a gang of painters was painting the underside of the platform canopy. Ladders and trestles on the platform edge were moved back to give clearance which gave me time for taking a photograph before we were on our way again.

The wagons loaded with materials were placed in Uxbridge Yard near the water tank but no water was available for L94. After running round the remainder of the train we set off on our return trip. Terry was concerned whether water would be available at Acton Town so he stopped at Rayners Lane to phone John who was once again charge driver at Lillie Bridge. John assured him that water was available and would not mean coming off our train.

When we reached Acton Town I went up to put the bag in the filling hole and saw that only one foot of water remained in the bottom of the tank, not quite enough to make it back to Lillie Bridge. The tanks replenished we made it back and disposed of the engine before going on our way. John was by now very interested in seeing the results of my photography and a visit to his home was arranged one evening with my slide projector, much to the amusement of his wife and children.

A night off midweek gave me another chance to join John and Terry on L94 working a train towards Hammersmith Metropolitan Line station. The work for the gangers meant a prolonged stop at Praed Street Junction where conversation started up again. John, like many of the drivers I had fired to at Stratford, was a good raconteur.

He recounted how small the cabs had been on the Peckett 0-6-0 saddle tanks, with their coal bunkers inside the cab, used mainly for shunting at Neasden Power Station. The subject then changed to early railway history and he pointed out that we were at an historic location. We left the cab and walked along the track to see where the broad and standard gauge converged, once called Bellmouth Junction, Praed Street – how

L90 stands at St Mary's Junction, Whitechapel whilst the P-Way gang were picking up worn rails during April 1970. *Gordon Wells*

A closer view of L90 whilst standing at St Mary's Junction. *Gordon Wells*

A final shot of L90 at St Mary's. The timed exposure gives a false impression of the amount of light available. The P-Way gang had to work by the light of Tilley lamps and the amount of infrastructure underfoot that had to be avoided whilst lifting heavy and awkward loads such as rail and sleepers can be appreciated from this view. A gang of 24 men was required to pick up a 60ft length of rail weighing about 80lbs per yard from ground level with at least 3-4 more men on the bolster wagon. The ganger in charge would call out his orders, the first being 'down', with the rider 'come along, spread yourselves out'. The skids were already fitted on the sole bar of the wagon and the next order was 'lift' and the rail would be lifted to knee height by the many hands and heaved onto the bottom bracket of the skid with much crashing as it landed. The next order would be 'push up' and with much shrieking of steel on steel the rail would be pushed up the skid and on to the floor of the wagon. Once on the floor the rail was levered across by the men on the bolster wagon with crow bars to make room for the next rail. In the dark the ganger would signal to the engine to move forward another 60ft to pick up the next length. This manhandling of rails was something I had not seen for a number of years on the main line where a handful of men achieved the same task with a number of small cranes mounted on the wagon itself.   *Gordon Wells*

confined the tunnels were when working a steam engine towards 'Jack's Wood' as he called St John's Wood.

It seemed no time at all before the gangers had finished their work and we were away to Hammersmith. Paddington station echoed back our exhaust as L94 climbed up from the tunnel onto the Hammersmith Line. No time for pictures as it was a quick run round and back to Lillie Bridge. Stopping L94 by the coal stage I assisted in shovelling half a ton or so. I may add that the coal supplied to London Transport was screened good quality Welsh navigation coal, virtually smokeless when burning, unlike the variable quality coal supplied to Stratford and its outstation depots with the implementation of the 1955 Clean Air Act, which ranged from large lumps which had to be broken to dusty 'fines'.

Other memories remain: travelling east with Terry driving and being held at Tower Hill station on a warm night waiting for an engineers' block to be lifted so that we could proceed; the undulating gradient profiles between stations with the dip

as we left one and the rise as we approached the next, most noticeable with a loose coupled train; standing on an eastbound train with John and Terry when the paraffin in the gauge lamp began to vaporise – the cure I suggested was a drop of engine oil in the paraffin which, despite John's fear for his lamp, worked; a trip back from Upminster where the trip cock arm caught on something and we were brought to a grinding halt at Dagenham East almost opposite a Class 31 shunting the coal yard, the driver looking over quizzically as John dropped down to reset the trip cock.

In early October 1970 L95 was confined to yard shunting having had her right driving wheel tyre work loose on the wheel centre. A weld repair enabled her to return to traffic. As winter approached increasing use of battery locomotives was made for working engineers' trains. The last note I have is of seeing L94 at Neasden and L90 and L95 at Lillie Bridge. So ended an episode that had enabled me to experience an Indian summer of steam, several years after its demise on BR.

L94 stands with its train at Ealing Broadway, the terminus of the District Line branch from Turnham Green through Acton Town. This trip was undertaken in the middle of 1970. *Gordon Wells*

L94 again at Ealing Broadway where, due to the amount of time spent standing there was ample opportunity for photography. On the footplate the open firebox doors allow the fire to cast a welcoming glow. *Gordon Wells*

L94 at Ealing Broadway waiting for the road to Lillie Bridge.

Gordon Wells

L94 pauses at Sudbury Hill on the Piccadilly Line with a train for Uxbridge. The stop was occasioned by a detonator being set off protecting a work gang on the platform.

Gordon Wells

A plume of smoke marks L94's presence in the yard at Lillie Bridge as viewed southwards from the Cromwell Road overbridge on the 15th March 1970. Some departmental stock stands alongside the parapet of the retaining wall above the curve of the District Line round to West Kensington which passes under the plate girder bridge. The cutting coming towards the camera takes the lines to Kensington Olympia. *Gordon Wells*

On the same occasion L94 is seen alongside the steam shed whilst shunting a pair of ballast wagons. The rails in the foreground are the West London Lines. *Gordon Wells*

L89 at Pinner Green returning to Neasden with a pair of empty wagons and two of the Ashford-built brake vans in May 1969.   *Keith Lawrence*

L95 approaching Harrow on the Hill on an engineering train. The remains of the Metropolitan goods yard can be seen on the right with some non-electrified sidings still in situ. The lines rising up are those of the burrowing junction for the Uxbridge Branch.   *Keith Lawrence*

L95 taking water at Watford whilst working the Watford Tip spoil train. The locomotive has been detached from the train to run round. A train of 'A' stock stands in the other platform.
Keith Lawrence

KEITH LAWRENCE

Back in 1968 I would go over to Watford and Croxley to take photographs as often as my shifts at Heathrow would permit. I came to be recognised by many of the crews on the panniers as they ran into Watford Metropolitan station sidings to take water, run round the stock and depart for Watford Tip.

Usually I would then follow them down to the tip or run on to various locations between Croxley and Harrow where, if the crews spotted me I would always get a cheery wave or a toot on the whistle as they ran back to Neasden.

Looking back over the years the thing I remember about the spoil trains to Croxley was the friendliness of the mainly West Indian train crews. I remember on one occasion, when I was taking photographs there on a cold February day in 1969 and up to my ankles in snow, the guard took pity on me and invited me up into his warm van as the loco ran the spoil train down to the end of the tip, a gesture I much appreciated.

Happy days indeed in a part of Britain devoid of steam traction over main running lines.

L95 leaves Watford for the tip at Croxley having run round its train and topped up with water.
Keith Lawrence

L95 crossing the Grand Union Canal just east of Watford South Junction.

Keith Lawrence

L94 at Watford Tip on a snowy day in February 1969. The photographer was soon to be invited into the welcome warmth of the brake van for the run down to the end of the sidings.

Keith Lawrence

The loaded wagons ready to be propelled down to the tip. Brake van B.555 is another built by Hurst, Nelson in 1935. *Keith Lawrence*

L95 in the tip sidings sorting out the wagons. The train's second brake van stands in front of the cranes. *Keith Lawrence*

A more unusual view at Watford Tip as L95 starts to sort the wagons.   *Keith Lawrence*

On a misty morning L90 comes off the main line at Watford South Junction heading for Watford prior to returning to the tip with a very lightly loaded train.   *Keith Lawrence*

Steam meets electric with L95 on the climb up to Northwood.

Keith Lawrence

Looking over the railway fence L89 is seen heading for the tip at Croxley.

Keith Lawrence

CHAPTER SIX
LONDON TRANSPORT STEAM SHEDS

LILLIE BRIDGE

Lillie Bridge was first used by the Metropolitan District Railway as a maintenance depot when they began to operate train services in their own right in 1871. Having severed the relationship with the Metropolitan Railway the District had to purchase its own locomotives and rolling stock and also to set up a repair and storage depot.

The depot was set up on land to the west of the curve from Earl's Court to the West London Railway and initially was connected only to the West London Railway thus necessitating a reversal to access the depot. The depot was completed in 1872 and in 1874 was also connected to the District's Hammersmith extension by means of a line down to West Kensington station.

With the electrification of the District in 1905 a new depot was established at Ealing Common (originally called Mill Hill Park Depot) and a large number of the District's steam locomotives were disposed of. From the fleet of fifty-four 4-4-0s to the same design as those on the Metropolitan, a total of six were kept for working engineering trains. These were retained at Lillie Bridge.

The site was radically altered in 1905-06 when a car shed for the new Great Northern, Piccadilly & Brompton Railway was built, access to which was via the line from West Kensington station. The rest of Lillie Bridge was retained by the District for engineering purposes. Of its locomotive fleet only two of the 4-4-0s survived beyond the Great War, one to 1925 and one to 1932. To replace them two 0-6-0 tanks were bought from the Hunslet Engine Co. in 1931. Numbered L30 and L31 (see page 16) they were the first to carry the 'L' prefix.

The scene at Lillie Bridge altered again in 1933 when the Piccadilly's depot at Cockfosters opened and the car shed at Lillie Bridge was vacated. The whole site was now given over to engineering purposes. From the depot the entire Underground network was serviced. The old car shed became home to some of the fleet of battery electric locomotives and to various service vehicles such as sleet cars.

From published photographic evidence it would appear that the steam shed seen here was a replacement structure. Certainly it has a fairly modern appearance being constructed of brick and corrugated sheeting with roller shutter doors and massive circular roof vents. Immediately in front of the two road shed was a water column serving both roads and a concrete coaling stage with bins for coal storage.

Above: L90 stands alongside the coal stage at Lillie Bridge. The shed beyond appears to be a replacement for an earlier structure on much the same site.
Kevin McCormack

Opposite: An unidentified pannier stands outside the shed.

Gordon Wells

Left: Panniers L92 (5786) and the second L90 (7760) at rest on Lillie Bridge shed 20th October 1966.
R. K. Blencowe

Below: A sketch plan of Lillie Bridge Depot showing the main layout of buildings as at the mid 1950s.

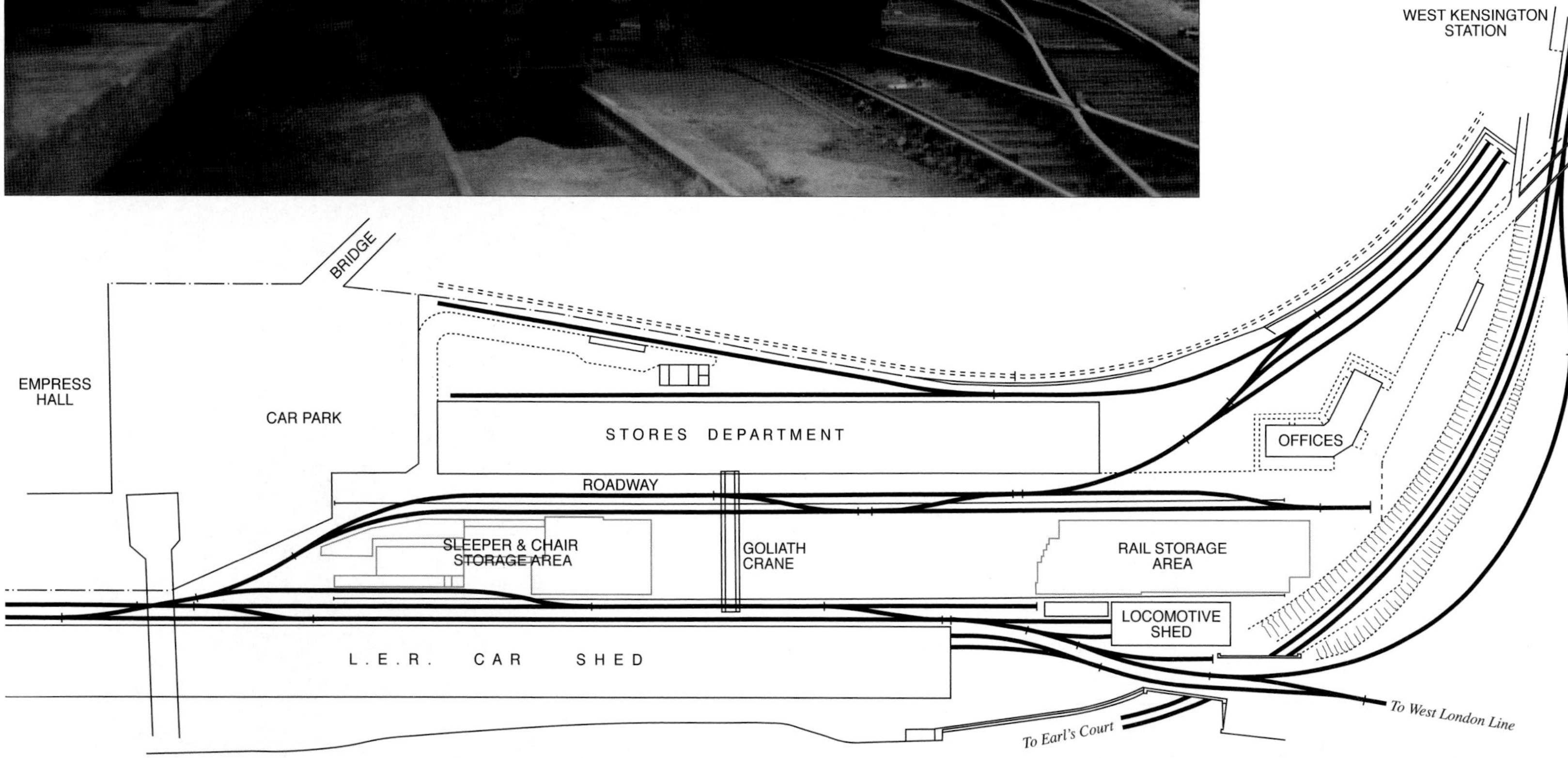

WEST KENSINGTON STATION

To West London Line

OFFICES

RAIL STORAGE AREA

LOCOMOTIVE SHED

To Earl's Court

STORES DEPARTMENT

GOLIATH CRANE

ROADWAY

SLEEPER & CHAIR STORAGE AREA

L. E. R.   C A R   S H E D

BRIDGE

CAR PARK

EMPRESS HALL

A general view of Lillie Bridge Depot as seen from the West Cromwell Road bridge in June 1969. On the left are the tracks of the West London Extension Joint Line (GWR, LNWR, LSWR & LBSCR Joint) with the sidings full of wagons overshadowed by the bulk of the Earls Court exhibition centre. A District Line train which has just left West Kensington station for Earls Court is diving under these tracks at what was known as West Kensington East Junction, now Olympia Junction, the low level lines in the foreground heading to Olympia. In the centre, London Transport ex-GWR 0-6-0PT No. L95 is propelling a works train into the yard of the depot, having just arrived from the Addison Road direction (now Kensington Olympia), while various battery electric locos stand around between duties. The four chimneys of the power station which was close by Wandsworth Bridge can be seen in the distance. This whole area is transformed today, much of it covered by the extension to the Earls Court exhibition complex, though some of the depot tracks are still in use.   *Geoff Plumb*

The skyline above Lillie Bridge Depot is dominated by the Empress State building as L90 shunts in the permanent way rail yard at the depot. The bridge in the left foreground with the Land Rover parked on it is over the District Line tracks near West Kensington station. June 1969.   *Geoff Plumb*

Two views of L95 on shed on the 10th June 1965. In the upper view it can be seen that one of the 6-ton diesel-electric cranes, either DEC617 or 618, built by Taylor & Hubbard in the mid 1950s is in for attention, its rear outline can just be discerned. *Keith Harwood*

Two night shots of panniers at Lillie Bridge. Above we see L94 on the 17th April 1970 whilst below an unidentified pannier stands under the glare of the shed's external lighting in the middle of 1971.

Gordon Wells

L98 stands alongside the coal stage at Lillie Bridge shed in the summer of 1968 whilst another unidentified pannier stands on the second road. The 1905 car shed can be seen beyond with some of the ubiquitous flat wagons in front, two of which carry cement mixers. *Kirk Martin*

Looking away from the shed entrance L95 stands alongside the coaling stage in early 1970. Note the fire devil to the left of the water column, an obviously 'home made' product in which a fire would be lit to keep the column from freezing in winter. *Gordon Wells*

Notices, lamps and steam – a very atmospheric view of a pannier front end at the entrance of Lillie Bridge shed. *Kirk Martin*

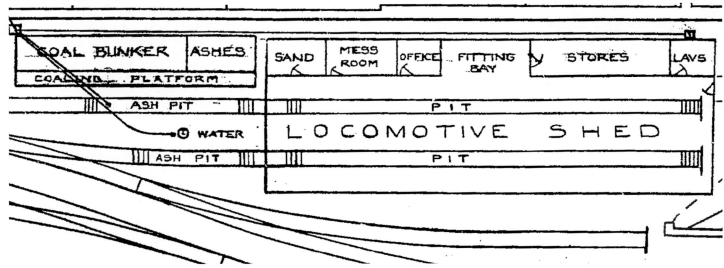

A plan of the shed, which measured some 140 feet by 50 feet, showing the various internal offices. *Transport for London Group Archives*

A rare view inside Lillie Bridge shed and workshop showing plant and machinery. Of the two sheds Lillie Bridge carried out heavier repairs as can be seen in this view with a pannier undergoing repair. Stood alongside are a set of jacks used for lifting the locos and they have been used in this case as the crank axle is out and stood in front of the engine. It could well be that the engine is L89 as it received attention to its bottom end and cylinders which involved the removal of the front buffer plank. This was then repainted and explains why in later images of L89 she has a bright red buffer plank. Note also the boiler tubes in the rack and two ballast hopper wagons undergoing maintenance on the left. *Kirk Martin*

L96 stands in the shed on the 20th October 1966. Another glimpse of the back of the shed is also gained where can be seen a number of machine tools to assist with general repairs. A ballast wagon also receives attention at the rear of the other road.

R. K. Blencowe

L94 inside the shed between turns, February 1970. Note that it is fitted with a pair of lamp brackets on the smokebox door. The reason for these being fitted to a single locomotive is unknown. They are suggestive of Southern Region practice and it could be that a replacement smokebox door was obtained from one of the '57XX' class that had been transferred to the Southern.

Gordon Wells

This shot of L95, taken on the 16th March 1967, gives a good view of the back of the shed. Note how, when compared with the view on page 51, the ground at the rear of the shed has been made up. Notice also the single electrified line into the depot, coming up from West Kensington. This gave access to the old car shed for such as sleet locomotives and other departmental stock.

R. K. Blencowe

Looking along the entrance road to the yard with L90 on the coaling stage.

Philip Fink

A final shot of Lillie Bridge looking into the yard past L98.

Kirk Martin

L97 stands at the southern end of Neasden steam shed on the 6th October 1968. Records show that at this date it was out of use having been withdrawn the previous month. The view gives a glimpse of something other than a steam locomotive in the shed. It is thought that it might well be one of the Plasser-Theurer tamping machines acquired in 1966.

Mike Morant

NEASDEN

From the early 1880s Neasden was home to the Metropolitan Railway's steam fleet. Originally facilities had been provided at Edgware Road but with developments and expansion they soon became far too cramped. In 1881 work began on a new site at Neasden where in 1883 a new locomotive works was opened. Here many of the Metropolitan's locomotive fleet were rebuilt and three members of the 'E' class were actually constructed.

On the same site was built a locomotive shed of wooden construction. It had two roads and held about ten locomotives. Others were shedded at various outstations such as New Cross, Chesham and Aylesbury. In 1898 the Neasden shed was replaced by a roundhouse with twice the capacity. Again, it was of wooden construction but was to have a relatively short life being demolished in 1908 when in a poor state of repair.

Rather than build yet another dedicated locomotive shed the steam locomotives were rehoused in three roads of the old carriage washing shed. This had been built in 1897 of corrugated iron construction.

This home served until the transfer of the larger locomotives and most of the Metropolitan steam hauled workings to the LNER in 1937. With a much reduced locomotive fleet dedicated mainly to engineering work the opportunity was taken to remodel the Neasden site and a new two road engine shed of brick construction was provided. It is this structure which is seen here. For some reason the old style of high coaling stage was retained, this had worked when coal wagons were unloaded from a siding within but as has been seen when serviced from a wagon at a lower level things were difficult.

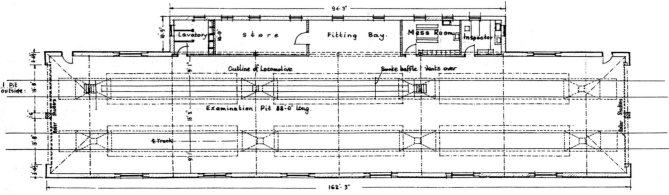

Neasden Shed floor plan, the main shed measured 162ft 3in. x 35ft 7in. with a store, fitting shop and the usual facilities in the block on the side.

Transport for London Group Archives

L94 and L92 on the Neasden coaling stage at the north end of the shed during the summer of 1969. Comparison with early views at this location will show the difference made to the skyline by the demolition of the power station.

Kevin McCormack

Two views taken on the 6th October 1968 with L90 nearest the camera. Both locomotives have marks on the leading splashers showing where the diamond-shaped North British builder's plates were fitted. By deduction therefore the furthest locomotive is L94 as it also has the smokebox door lamp brackets fitted as seen previously.

Mike Morant

A further group of panniers at the north end of the shed with L97 in the front and L92 left rear. Notice that L97 exhibits a variation in the pipework to the trip cock as it runs below the valence and appears to go much lower behind the step. *J. E. Connor*

The southern end of the shed appears to have been rarely photographed so this view of L94 stood outside is particularly useful. It does show the rather utilitarian 1930s design of the structure – serving its purpose and no more. As with Lillie Bridge roller shutter doors are fitted. *J. E. Comnor*

An outstanding view inside Neasden shed with four panniers at home. The only one that can be identified with certainty is L94 on the right by virtue of the smokebox door lamp brackets. The loco on the left appears to have lost its steam lance take-off cock on the smokebox front. Notice also the fire devil, probably used to keep the shed warm.

Two views inside the Neasden steam shed with L92, L94 and one other present. The shed has the usual clutter around the edges, including a staff member's bicycle, but the middle between the two roads is commendably clear. L92 has had a patch put on the lower half of its tank, hence the missing patch of lining. Panniers were prone to rusting through here and some are seen with a patch or new portion welded in place along the entire lower half of the tank, L89 being an example of this. Whilst undated the photographs predate the fitting of the train reporting code brackets but L92 and L94 both sport sleet brush brackets and L94 has yet to gain extra lamp brackets.

R. A. Simpson, courtesy Colin Judge

L94 and L95 stand on the right with an unidentified shedmate on the left.

Mike Morant

L90 stands in pools of sunlight entering through the shed windows in May 1971.

Ron Head

Four panniers are visible in this interior view at Neasden, 1968. What is apparent on L95 is the degree to which the dirt could be polished! It certainly gave the locomotives a distinctive patina.
Mike Morant

SOME MEMORIES OF A STEAM APPRENTICE
by Ron Head

I started my career with London Transport in the apprentice training centre at Acton Works, in 1968 – the same year that BR finished with steam for good. It was customary for Acton apprentices to be sent to a depot for a spell, and in my case, I had the good fortune to spend the winter of 1969/70 at Neasden.

Neasden Depot was an interesting place to work, because it was responsible for both surface and tube stock, and of course a small steam fleet, which by that time had been reduced to just six engines. Part of my time was spent doing shed-day exams and programmed lifts on the electric stock, and the rest was spent in the steam shed, where I got to know many of the characters employed there.

The winter was bitterly cold, with snow on the ground for much of the time, and it was a treat to go into the steam shed for a warm-up by the huge coal fired stove that stood between the two roads in the shed. I worked mostly with Bill Standen, a time-served fitter who had come across from the Great Central shed at Neasden when it closed. Bill was a master of his trade, but unfortunately his mate had no enthusiasm for the job and so I often took his place. Bill introduced me to the art of packing piston and valve glands on an inside-cylindered engine, and I will never forget standing in a pit under an engine in steam, trying to wield spanners in a confined space, whilst enduring a constant hot shower from the leaking steam that was condensing on the underside of the boiler.

I also spent some time helping Bill Craigh, the boilersmith. His life was made miserable by one engine in particular – L89

– which was always in trouble with one boiler problem or another. We expanded the tubes and caulked the firebox seams on several occasions to try to stem weeps, all carried out inside a hot boiler. In the end some stays were deemed to be fractured and had to be drilled out and replaced 'blind' – that is, with access from the fire side only, and this required great skill on Bill's part. At times like these, I realised why steam just wasn't viable for LT any longer.

On a couple of occasions I sneaked a ride on the daily Watford Tip run with driver Ray Woods, which was a magical experience in the frosty winter atmosphere. I was also allowed to move the engines on shed, under the watchful eye of George Freshwater, the genial locomotive inspector, who took a kindly interest in me. I well remember being shown how to light an engine up by charge driver Harry Varley; first a layer of coal went in, followed by several bundles of old traffic circulars. The whole lot was doused with a bucket of paraffin, a lighted match was

thrown in and the firedoors were quickly slammed shut. I don't recall firewood being used on these occasions.

I was surprised to find that the term 'pannier tank' wasn't generally used on LT, and the engines were usually referred to as 'Westerns' by the staff, to differentiate them from the old 'Met' engines, which were still fondly remembered. I spent many hours around the stove, mug of tea in hand, listening to tales of the 'E's, 'F's and 'humpty dumpties' [the Pecketts]. The engines were kept continuously in steam, even when there was no work for them, the fires being dropped only when boiler washouts became due. The fire would be pulled back into a heap just under the firehole door, and a couple of large fresh lumps would be added every few hours. With the blower turned off and the rear damper open, the engine would happily sit with around 50 p.s.i. on the 'clock' until it was required again.

I eventually returned to Acton for a spell in the drawing office, but I always made a point of watching out for the daily steam

Boiler inspector William Criagh of Neasden is seen inspecting the boiler tubes inside the shed at Neasden. This illustration was used in July 1968 in a feature on the pannier tanks in *London Transport Magazine*. *courtesy London Transport Museum*

Two views of L94 undergoing its last overhaul at Ealing Common Depot in February 1971. This is the only time that a steam locomotive was lifted on the hydraulic jacks which had been provided for the overhaul of battery locomotives.
Ron Head

trip working from Lillie Bridge to Acton, Ealing Common and Northfields, which passed by the office window.

When the day came for the 'farewell to steam' open day at Neasden on the 6th June 1971, I volunteered to act as a guide, and was able to witness L94 arriving with the last steam hauled engineers' train from Moorgate. It then spent the afternoon shuttling up and down the Klondyke sidings for the benefit of the cameras, in company with L90 at the other end of the train. The third surviving engine at this time, L95, was back at the shed, having been retired some days earlier due to loose tyres on the trailing axle. At the end of the afternoon, the two engines were coupled together and ran 'light' back to the shed, accompanied by a prolonged bout of farewell whistling.

My duties over for the day, I went up to the shed to see the fires being dropped for the last time. It was sad to think that a whole era had come to an end, but comforting to know that the engines were to be spared from the breaker's torch. When all seemed to be over, someone had the idea of driving L90 up to the exit point and back to the shed on the remaining steam in the boiler. I climbed aboard for what was undoubtedly the last movement of a steam loco in working service on LT.

Looking back, I'm proud to say that I was probably one of the last apprentices to be trained on everyday working steam, anywhere in the country, and I was later to put my accumulated knowledge to good use in the preservation world – but that is another story.

L92 on Neasden coaling stage in the summer of 1969. The height of the stage is apparent in this view, which, whilst making it easier to fill locomotive bunkers made restocking the stage from mineral wagons far more difficult. One wonders if the height was a throwback to the old Metropolitan coal stage where coal wagons were taken in at a higher level as just apparent at the top of page 17.
Kevin McCormack

A more unusual view towards the shed off the coal stage looking over the tanks and a well-filled bunker.
P. Watson

Taken on a shed visit to Neasden, possibly on an open day, is this view of a pair of panniers on the coaling stage, looking in the opposite direction to that in the lower picture on the previous page.
Tim Mead

An atmospheric steamy view of the bunkers of L92 and L89 as they stand alongside the coal stage at Neasden – note the tail lamps and the fire irons resting on the brackets on the bunkers.
Kirk Martin

Two bunker views of pristine panniers at Neasden on the 10th June 1965, both at the north end of the shed, conclude the look at Lillie Bridge and Neasden sheds. L93 stands on the coal stage road whilst L89 is on shed with George Freshwater in shirtsleeves discussing some point with a member of staff.
Keith Harwood

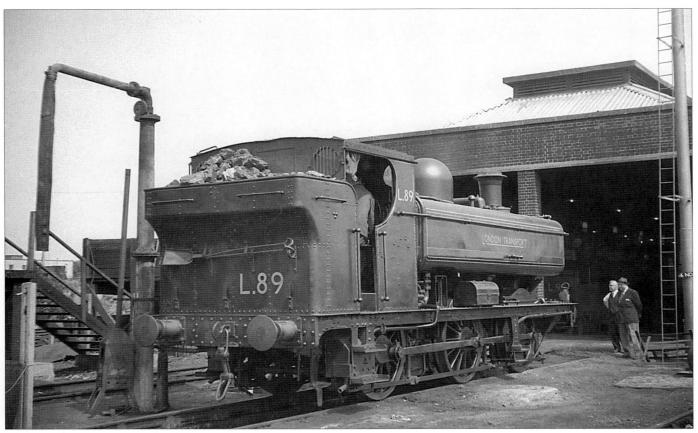

An evocative night-time shot of three panniers, cold on the siding at Neasden awaiting their fate.

Awaiting the end at Neasden on the 6th November 1969 were L98 (7739), L91 (5757) and L97 (7749). After parts were removed for further use all three panniers were cut up on site during 1970 having been officially withdrawn in January.   *photographer unknown*

CHAPTER SEVEN
THE LAST DAYS

The panniers continued in their work, mainly on the Watford Tip workings from Neasden and on material and equipment transfers between Lillie Bridge and Acton Works, throughout the 1960s. There were also the engineering train workings and occasional forays with the breakdown train on top of the yard shunting at both Lillie Bridge and Neasden.

As has been seen, the last days for two of the panniers came sooner than expected. Both the first L90 (7711) and L91 (5752) had short LT service lives, L90 between October 1956 and September 1961, and L91 between February 1957 and November 1960, both were exchanged with BR for replacements.

The pannier fleet soldiered on with their duties until mechanical failure or boiler problems forced their withdrawal, a situation that became more acute after the end of steam on British Railways Western Region and the cessation of steam repair work at Swindon. The first to go in September 1967 was L96 which, like many of its former BR sisters, was cut up by the scrap dealers Cashmores. One reason for its demise was the availability of a number of newer battery locomotives freed up from the construction works on the Victoria Line.

Exactly one year later L93 was withdrawn and again was cut up at Neasden by Cashmores. L92 was the next to succumb in October 1969 but was to have a further lease of life as it was sold to the Worcester Locomotive Preservation Society who moved it to their site at Hereford.

1970, always given as the final year for the operation of the pannier tanks, saw a decimation of the remaining locomotives. In January L89, L91, L97, L98 and L99 were all officially withdrawn. L91, L97 and L98 were all cut up at Neasden by the Steel Breaking & Dismantling Company of Sheffield. L89 and L99 were thankfully to survive, L89 going to the Keighley & Worth Valley Railway (later to feature in The Railway Children) and L99 remained on Metropolitan territory going to Quainton Road having been bought by the London Railway Preservation Society.

This left three panniers in service and they survived for a further year. Steam hauled Acton Works stores trains ceased in February 1971 and then the Watford Tip workings went over to haulage by the battery locomotives. The last revenue trip for a pannier was worked between Lillie Bridge and Neasden on the 4th June by L90 – although the occasion was marred by the dropping of a fusible plug and subsequent rescue by a battery locomotive.

Two days later a special train from Moorgate to Neasden with L94 was operated to officially celebrate the end of steam on London Transport. The train consisted of a sample of the engineering wagons associated with the panniers. In conjunction with the event an open day was held at Neasden where L90 was also in steam (despite the disgrace of two days earlier) and there was a display of rolling stock and the Sentinel diesels that were to replace the panniers. Some 8,500 people attended the open day, about 2,000 of whom had travelled in special trains behind L94 and its demonstration train.

Thus a fitting end was given to both the pannier tanks that had served for almost fifteen years with LT and steam on the Metropolitan and District lines which stretched back to 1863.

With only a month to go before the end of steam on London Transport L94 was photographed at Lillie Bridge on the 15th April 1971.   *G. Moon*

Two views of L93 and an unidentified stable mate in the scrap line at Neasden. Note that L93 has lost the handrail from along the pannier tank. Other fittings have probably been removed, some to keep shedmates operative. *above, P. Watson; below, Mike Morant*

One wonders what the thoughts were as staff look on at pannier L93 being cut up at Neasden in September 1968. With his foot on the rail is fitter Bill Standen whilst on the right appears to be driver Richard Cox. In the view below the lining on the tank makes a useful cutting guide whilst the bunker sits at an angle the footplate having been cut through.   *Kirk Martin*

Tubes litter the yard alongside the smokebox from which the cast chimney has been broken. A sister locomotive lurks in the background awaiting its similar fate. *Kirk Martin*

Below: The second L91 stands forlornly at the back of Neasden Yard awaiting transportation to the scrap yard early in 1970. Parts have already been removed such as the safety valve cover, the injector and the trip cock, also the smokebox door handles hence no doubt the string to stop the door flying open en route. *Ron Head*

THE LAST NIGHTLY RUN
by Ken Mumford

The night of Friday/Saturday May 14th/15th 1971 was to be the last night that London Transport was going to operate a steam locomotive on a permanent way train. At about 00.15 on the Saturday morning L90 left Lillie Bridge steam depot for its last nightly run to Neasden Depot via Rayners Lane. Its route would be over the District and Piccadilly lines to Ealing Common, then up the Piccadilly Line to Rayners Lane, where the locomotive would run around its train, then down the Metropolitan Line to Neasden Depot.

We parked in a rather well-to-do residential cul-de-sac near Sudbury, Middlesex as one of the residents was about to exercise his dog. He was a little suspicious of us. I mean, who in their right mind would be up at around midnight watching trains? In fact, he didn't believe us at first. I don't know if he believed us in the end!

Very few people knew about this run. Six of those who did made for a footbridge situated between Sudbury Town and Sudbury Hill stations. This footbridge was ideally situated. Just the place to tape-record and photograph the steam train as it climbed up the steep gradient between the two stations. Arriving at the footbridge at about half past midnight, the last three Piccadilly Line trains were observed – the last to Barons Court, the last to Rayners Lane and the last to South Harrow – before the sound of a steam locomotive working hard could be heard in the distance. This was the signal to switch on the tape-recorder and to get camera equipment ready.

Into sight came the little pannier tank hauling two brake vans and two loaded ballast wagons. As the gradient steepened approaching the footbridge, the driver opened the regulator to give more power, its exhaust bark became louder and at the same time caused the locomotive to emit more dirty white exhaust. No lights, however, go on in the houses that back on to the line.

The train stormed under the footbridge and that unique smell filled one's nostrils as the exhaust hung under the bridge. Cameras clicked, flash-bulbs popped and the tape-recorders remained on even when the steam train had disappeared from sight until the sound of it working hard as it climbed the gradient could not be heard anymore. Then there was a mad dash to the cars – no time to put the equipment away properly – then a quick journey to Rayners Lane Underground station in time to see the locomotive run around its train in the station yard. There was also a chance to take some more photographs and to do some tape-recording as the locomotive ran around its train before setting off down the Metropolitan Line to Neasden Depot.

There was another three and a half hours before L90 and its train arrived back at Rayners Lane station from Neasden Depot on its journey back to Lillie Bridge. We decided to kill that time by having a look at Stonebridge Park bus depot. Here we were allowed to satisfy our hunger by using the machines in the staff canteen. There was still some time left before we needed to return to see L90 again at Rayners Lane, so we went around to have a look at Neasden Depot from the iron girder bridge over the North Circular Road which was very deserted at 03.00 in the morning. From the bridge we could see, in the distance by means of the depot's lights, a plume of steam rising from the safety valves of

It was to L90 that the honour of working the last Lillie Bridge to Neasden train fell on the night of the 14th/15th May 1971. Sadly no images taken on that occasion have been found so this one of L90 in Neasden Yard has to suffice. *courtesy London Transport Museum*

L94 is seen working past Ravenscourt Park with brake van B.553 in June 1970.

Geoff Plumb

L90. As we could not enter the depot because of the electrified lines, we made our way back to the station car park at Rayners Lane. Some of us tried to get a short nap in our cars.

About four in the morning it began to get light. The birds greeted the dawn by singing in the trees that surrounded the station car park. Station staff started arriving – the signalman going to open his box to allow the first train of the day (a Metropolitan Line train bound for Baker Street) to enter the station. This was the signal to get our photographic and tape-recording equipment ready. A Piccadilly Line train bound for Barons Court arrived and then departed, another Metropolitan train for Baker Street, then the signal at the western end of Rayners Lane turned from red to green which indicated that our steam train was about to enter the station.

Tape-recorders were switched on, cameras were at the ready as L90 puffed into the station. It proceeded beyond the station in order to set back into the station yard where it ran around its train (the ballast wagons now being empty) then propelled it out of the yard back onto the main line then whistled to the signalman who set the road for L90 to take the Piccadilly line at the junction on the east side of the station. As the steam locomotive accelerated through the station it left a long thick trail of dirty white exhaust across the station platforms and showered the enthusiasts with smuts and a fine spray of dirty water from its exhaust. The tape-recorders remained on until the steam locomotive could not be heard anymore – steam had left Rayners Lane forever. Six, very tired, but well satisfied, transport enthusiasts then made their way home – and bed.

A snap from low-level of L94 paused at Rayners Lane.

Gordon Wells

At Barbican station eight minutes were allowed as a photo opportunity and the platforms were packed. The crowds were soon to be treated to the sounds of a Great Western exhaust echoing off the brick retaining walls as L94 pulled away for Neasden. *courtesy London Transport Museum*

L94 emerges into the daylight at Farringdon. *Geoff Plumb*

L94 and train departs the crowded platforms at Farringdon whilst a few souls look over the retaining wall. The train was comprised a 1935 Hurst, Nelson brake van B.557; rail wagon RW473; flat wagon F348, of the kind so often seen on Watford Tip workings; cable wagon F348 a converted flat wagon; diesel crane C617 and jib carrier J688; ballast wagon HW428; and finally a 1962 Ashford built brake van B.582.   *Andy Sturt*

THE FINAL FAREWELL

As the public became increasingly aware of the impending end of London Transport steam there was an awakening of interest and many requests to visit the last steam sheds operating standard gauge steam in normal service in the country. People were eager to visit the sheds at Lillie Bridge and Neasden to see and photograph the last three surviving panniers.

The Railway Correspondence & Travel Society requested a special passenger train, which the Executive had to turn down owing to the fact that London Transport had removed the vacuum brake equipment from the pannier tanks as the locomotives were only used on shunting and engineers' trains and only required the steam brake on the engine. The RCTS had suggested that London Transport should acquire some vacuum brake equipment from stored locomotives at Woodham Brother's scrap yard at Barry in South Wales, to run such a train. The cost of this for just one rail tour was of course prohibitive.

In a letter to the RCTS Mr F. R. Wilkins, Chief Publicity Officer, stated that London Transport were formulating plans for a demonstration engineers' train after steam traction had officially finished on London Transport to give enthusiasts the chance to take photographs of this type of train before the last panniers were withdrawn from service. In a reply to Mr Wilkins the RCTS Rail Tours Officer, Mr J. Faithfull, stated his disappointment at London Transport's reluctance to run a passenger train for enthusiasts.

Right: 'Farewell to Steam'.   *courtesy London Transport Museum*

Farewell to Steam
ON THE UNDERGROUND

On Sunday, June 6 the last of the long line of standard-gauge steam locomotives which have served the Underground since 1863 will make a farewell run on the Metropolitan Line. For the last 10 years these engines have been used solely to haul London Transport works trains and for shunting in depots.

The special commemorative 'run' will take place during the afternoon from Moorgate to Neasden Depot. The train, hauled by a veteran 0-6-0 tank locomotive, will include many rarely-seen wagons.

A Souvenir Ticket (£1; children under 14, 50p) will be issued in limited numbers to admit you to the platforms at Barbican or Farringdon, where you are invited to photograph this unique event. It also entitles you to ride in a special follow-up train running directly to Neasden, and gives you unlimited travel for the day on Underground trains. Afterwards there is an Open Day featuring old and new Underground rolling stock at Neasden Depot, to which the Souvenir Ticket gives admission.

Come and pay your respects at the end of an era.
Apply for your tickets by writing to the London Transport Fares Office, 55 Broadway, S.W.1.
You must apply beforehand (with remittance).
Remember, numbers have to be strictly limited and applications must be dealt with on a 'first come, first served' basis.

A special full colour souvenir booklet 'The Last Drop' will be on sale (50p) at the show.

1863-1971

However, the RCTS letter must have had some effect as London Transport decided that something had to be done to commemorate the end of steam traction and as suggested in the letter from the RCTS some sort of rolling stock exhibition might be appropriate at a goods yard or depot. In the RCTS letter it was suggested that Metropolitan locomotive No. 1 should take part in the display as well as more recent rolling stock.

A possible site for the exhibition was Harrow on the Hill goods yard which, although closed, still had tracks in situ. In the event this suggestion was rejected although an event did take place at Neasden on the final day of steam on Sunday the 6th June 1971.

Prior to the run the wagons had been worked to Moorgate by battery locomotives and the train is seen here heading south through Willesden Green. *Keith Robertson*

THE LAST DAY
JOHN SCOTT-MORGAN

A special time table was arranged by the Office of the Superintendent (Traffic) for the occasion of the final working of a pannier hauled engineers' train. London Transport sold special red coloured travel cards with a pannier tank logo printed in white. These doubled up as a travel card for all lines on that date and also gave entry to the rolling stock exhibition at Neasden. The crowds on that day had to be seen to be believed! The platforms at stations along the Widened Lines from Moorgate to Farringdon were a heaving mass of people all pushing and jostling for any space to gain a vantage point to see and photograph the last train and to say a farewell to an elusive part of London Transport history.

My journey started at 11.00 on that bright sunny morning from Acton Town station. I was accompanied by my friend Derick Foster, from Manchester, who was a student in his final year at college in London. We travelled by Piccadilly Line to Hammersmith where we crossed over the road to the Metropolitan station taking a 'C69' stock train to Barbican station where we both purchased a copy of *The Last Drop*, a commemorative booklet from a sales table on the station concourse. This was very good value at fifty pence.

We managed to find a vantage point at the platform edge at the western end of the station where we waited for the last rites of London steam to take place. As we waited the feeling of anticipation rose amongst the people on the platform, some of whom had even brought along step ladders or even perched themselves on lamp posts and the steps of the signal box. The final train had already run through from Neasden to Moorgate by

L94 running light through Barbican on the way to Moorgate. It was crewed by driver Leslie Waring and fireman Nathan Francis. *P. Watson*

Some of those who made it possible.

Left: George Freshwater, the last steam inspector. Although he trained as a mechanical instrument maker he spent almost forty years involved with steam.

Above: Two of the oldest serving members of staff, Harry Varley of Neasden (left) and Harry Capel of Lillie Bridge with over sixty years of footplate experience between them.

Below: Fitter Bill Standen (left) and fitter's mate Frederick Lampard prepared L94 for the ceremonial run.

The special coasts in to its photographic stop at Barbican passing between the lines of spectators on the platforms.

Keith Robertson

The last train emerged into daylight again at Finchley Road.   *Lens of Sutton Association*

the time we arrived and all we had to do was await the final appearance of this historic train.

At last L94 appeared in a cloud of white vapour from the tunnel at the eastern end of the station and rolled through the non-electrified tracks on the south side of Barbican station, pausing only briefly before blowing a farewell blast on its whistle and departing through the gloom of the westbound tunnel on its historic journey to Neasden via Farringdon where the train would change over to the Circle Line and continue via Baker Street and the Metropolitan Main Line, via a brief stop at Finchley Road before switching to the Bakerloo Line to gain access to the exhibition at Neasden Depot.

Derick and I caught the first of two special trains of 'C69' stock from Barbican to Neasden which ran direct, arriving at 14.28. At the depot entrance there were large crowds of people waiting to enter the exhibition and it took a long time to reach the entrance gates. Eventually we managed to enter the crowded site and see just what London Transport had brought together for this historic event.

Along one siding there was a line of newly overhauled service stock including a battery locomotive, a sleet locomotive and the Metropolitan Railway electric locomotive No. 12 *Sarah Siddons*. Nearby there was a two car train of Metropolitan 'T' stock which was in use as a sleet train at Rickmansworth.

In the main depot building were examples of every type of rolling stock from each of the LT lines and a number of earlier types of passenger stock, painted chocolate brown, in departmental use. At the back of the main building a large number of people had gathered around a newly refurbished Rolls Royce engined 0-6-0 Sentinel diesel hydraulic locomotive.

Tomorrow, when all the fuss was over and all the crowds had gone, these secondhand diesels would inherit the panniers' domain. But now, for just a few hours, the panniers were the true stars of the show. Derick and I departed at around 17.00 and headed for home. It had been a

At 15.00 the special train arrived at Neasden and welcoming crowds can be seen lining the overbridge and in the yard beyond.   *P. Watson*

L90 was also in steam at Neasden and was attached to the train once it arrived in the yard.

Tim Mead

L94 was detached at the other end of the train and handed over to relief driver Donald Hourien, seen here stood close to the locomotive. All members of the footplate crews were asked to sign the souvenir booklets.

Keith Robertson collection

L90 took over the train at Neasden and is seen amongst the sea of Open Day visitors.
courtesy London Transport Museum

truly fine wake and yet, somehow, a sad day. I contemplated what life would be like without the sound of the pannier tanks echoing across West London at 01.00 on a winter's morning and recalled all those times I had a fleeting glimpse of a red pannier as my Underground train rattled along – a sight no more to be seen from this day.

But every cloud has a silver lining and for the three surviving panniers, there would be a new dawn. L90 (7760) which was in the worst condition, was sold to the Steel Breaking & Dismantling Company for scrap but had a reprieve when the Tyseley Railway Museum purchased her for preservation along with L94 (7752) which had hauled the last official train. L95 (5764) was sold to the Severn Valley Railway for preservation.

In all six of the thirteen panniers survive today in preservation, a testament to the last stand of steam on London Transport and, occasionally, have been seen once more running on their former London Transport routes.

EPILOGUE
On the last day, after the crowds had gone,
and after the fires had been drawn
and thrown out for the final time,
the red panniers stood in the shed,
their boilers cooling down slowly.
There would be no more red ghosts in the night in London.

JSM

Right: A leaflet was produced for the Open Day which gave details of the stock on display and also that in the final train. The event was also advertised by means of a poster similar in design as that for the Farewell to Steam, this gave the admission charge to the depot as being 20p.
Ron Head collection

Farewell to Steam

1863 - 1971

Display of Steam Train and other Rolling Stock at Neasden Depot
Sunday June 6, 1971, from 14 30 to 17 30
(NO ADMISSION AFTER 17 00)

Taken from a similar vantage point are the old and the replacement motive power. The view of L95 shows interesting detail on the top of the tanks and shows that they were rarely cleaned. A lot of this material was blasted off the tunnel roofs by the blast up the chimney and could cause problems. It is remembered that one locomotive suffered with brake problems and so a day was spent changing the vacuum brake cylinder but to no avail. It was found that the problem was actually caused by blocked holes in the blower ring in the smokebox caused by debris falling in. The solution – a straightened shunter's pole used like a toothpick down the chimney to poke the holes out!

Below is one of the battery locomotives, L36, that in part replaced the panniers' duties. L36 had been built by the Gloucester Railway Carriage & Wagon Co. in 1938 and entered service in March of that year. *both Geoff Plumb*

The direct replacements were the three Rolls-Royce engined Sentinel 0-6-0 diesels obtained from Charles Hill of Rotherham and numbered DL81-83. They had originally been built in 1967 for use at the Corby opencast iron ore workings in Northamptonshire. Above is DL81 the first to arrive in March 1971. The wheelbase was insufficient to operate the track circuits when out on the main line and so the tender had to be provided on which was also mounted the trip cock. These were constructed from 'Q' stock trailer bogies. Both the locomotive and the tender carry conventional coupling gear and also the Ward-Lock coupling allowing them to shunt other Underground stock. The Ward couplers were difficult to fit and their use precluded normal buffers being fitted to the Sentinel and so wooden dumb buffers were fitted at the front as seen below.   *Colour Rail*

Left. Two views of DL82 at Lillie Bridge Depot on the 11th June 1971, six days after the end of London Transport steam.   *G. Moon*

Above: A slight livery change is exhibited in this view of DL82 taken at Neasden in November 1978, the red buffer beams having been replaced by black and yellow chevrons.   *Cliff Baker/Ben Pope collection*

PANNIERS IN PRESERVATION

A medley of panniers in preservation. Over the years on their various lines they have gone through a variety of guises, carrying GWR and BR liveries with, just occasionally an appearance in LT red. They have now spent longer running in preservation than with London Transport. Most, if not all, are still easily identifiable as being ex-London Transport in that they have all retained the cab roof alteration with the overhang removed at the sides and the rainstrip angle moved further up the roof. All also have odd extra holes in the valence and front footsteps where the trip cocks were once fitted.

THE PHOTOGRAPHS

Top of page, left: Both L90 and L94 are seen here at Tyseley, Birmingham, soon after delivery from LT.   *Keith Robertson*
Top of page, right: L94 now restored to its original identity of 7752 is seen in 1946 GWR livery at a Tyseley open day.   *P. Watson*

Left, upper: L95 running light on the Severn Valley Railway.
Keith Robertson
Left, lower: Now restored as 5764 it prepares to leave Bridgnorth.
Keith Robertson

Bottom of page, left: 5786 (L92) at rest under the water column at Buckfastleigh on the South Devon Railway.   *Brian Croker*
Bottom of page, right: 5786 in a very rural setting crossing the River Dart on 'Nursery Pool' bridge.   *Brian Croker*

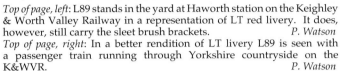

Top of page, left: L89 stands in the yard at Haworth station on the Keighley & Worth Valley Railway in a representation of LT red livery. It does, however, still carry the sleet brush brackets. *P. Watson*

Top of page, right: In a better rendition of LT livery L89 is seen with a passenger train running through Yorkshire countryside on the K&WVR. *P. Watson*

Right, upper: L89 is probably the best known of the ex-LT panniers, and possibly the best-known of all panniers, through its role in the film of *The Railway Children* when carrying a fictitious umber livery but still with sleet brush brackets. *P. Watson*

Right, lower: As with all of the six preserved panniers L89 has also carried its original GWR livery during preservation. *P. Watson*

Bottom of page, left: The closest to home, still on Metropolitan territory is 7715 seen here in all-over black at the Quainton Road home of the Buckinghamshire Railway Centre. *Keith Robertson*

Bottom of page, right: It is a pity that L99 does not stay in LT livery permanently at Quainton Road. Notice that between the dates of the two views the panniers have been replaced thus losing the tell-tale Kerr Stuart rivetted panels. *P. Watson*

Smaller items have also been preserved including some of the builder's plates and a number of the original GWR cab side plates that the locomotives arrived on LT with. *A. Delicata*

The LT metals had, however, not seen the last of the pannier tanks as they returned for the 'Steam on the Met' events in June 1993. *Above*: L90 and L99 are seen together near Moor Park whilst below L99 is seen on its own at West Kensington on District lines and very close to its old home at Lillie Bridge whilst working 'Steam on the District'.

both R. C. Stumpf

Also on the District in 1993 L99 is seen near Barons Court (above) with a Piccadilly Line train entering the tube tunnel to Earl's Court. L99 is seen again at Ealing Broadway (below) between a Central Line train on the right and District Line 'D78' stock beyond. *both R. C. Stumpf*

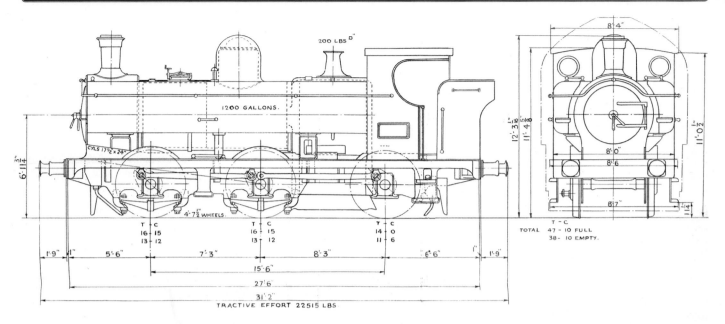

An outline drawing of a '57XX' pannier prepared by London Transport in April 1957 as drawing number 39179, traced from a Western Region print of the GWR 'weight diagram'. Originally drawn at $^3/_8$in. to 1 foot it has been reduced here to 4mm to 1 foot.

An interesting comparison with the weight diagram above is this side view of the first L90 (7711) when fresh out of the paint shop. Photographed at Neasden it is likely that the repaint took place there although later the panniers were known to have been repainted at Lillie Bridge. It is recognisable as a Kerr Stuart product by the rivetted tanks and the oval builder's plate on the leading splasher.

London Transport official, collection Ron Head

APPENDIX ONE
LOCOMOTIVE HISTORIES

L89 (5775)

Date	GWR/BR Shed allocation
1929	Built GWR, Swindon
1929	Into service, Neath
1930	Neath; Glyn Neath (Dec.)
1931	Glyn Neath; Neath & Brecon (May)
1932	Neath; Neath & Brecon (Sept.)
1933	n/a
1934	Neath
1935	Neath and Neath & Brecon (alternating)
1936	Neath and Neath & Brecon (alt.) and Glyn Neath
1937	Neath and Neath & Brecon (alt.)
1938	Neath and Neath & Brecon (alt.)
1939	Neath and Neath & Brecon (alt.)
1940	Neath and Neath & Brecon (alt.)
1941	Danygraig
1942	Danygraig
1943	Danygraig
1944	Danygraig
1945	Danygraig
1946	Danygraig
1947	Danygraig
1948	Danygraig
1949	Danygraig
1950	Danygraig
1951	Danygraig
1952	Danygraig; Carmarthen (Nov.)
1953	Carmarthen
1954	Carmarthen
1955	Carmarthen
1956	Carmarthen; Pontypool Road (March)
1957	Pontypool Road
1958	Pontypool Road
1959	Pontypool Road
1960	Pontypool Road
1961	Pontypool Road
1962	Pontypool Road
1963	Pontypool Road transferred (Feb.) LT

To London Transport 08.08.63
Withdrawn 20.01.70

Preserved   Keighley & Worth Valley Railway

5775 as L89 at Neasden shed c1968. It is possible to see what alterations were made by LT. The vacuum and steam heat pipes have been removed/blanked off, the smokebox numberplate has been replaced by indicator brackets for train reporting numbers and sleet brush fitting brackets have been added.
Kirk Martin

5775 at Old Oak Common Yard c1935 in its original condition as built.   *Rail Archive Stephenson*

5775 on the coaling stage, probably at Pontypool Road, in 1960 and finished in late BR livery.
Lens of Sutton Association

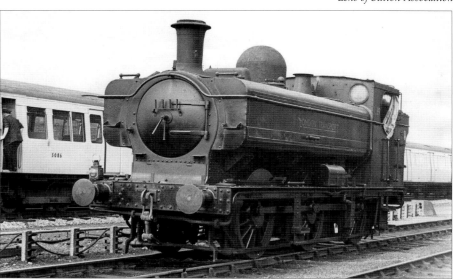

L90 [1] (7711)

Date	GWR/BR Shed allocation
1930	Built Kerr Stuart, Stoke on Trent
1930	Into service June Old Oak Common
1931	Old Oak Common
1932	Old Oak Common
1933	n/a
1934	Westbury (alt. with Salisbury & Frome)
1935	Westbury
1936	Westbury; Swindon (Dec.)
1937	Swindon
1938	Swindon
1939	Swindon
1940	Swindon
1941	Swindon; St Philip's Marsh (July)
1942	St Philip's Marsh (& occasionally Bath for a month)
1943	St Philip's Marsh (& occasionally Bath for a month)
1944	St Philip's Marsh (& occasionally Bath for a month)
1945	St Philip's Marsh (& occasionally Bath for a month)
1946	St Philip's Marsh (& occasionally Bath for a month)
1947	St Philip's Marsh (& occasionally Bath for a month)
1948	St Philip's Marsh
1949	St Philip's Marsh
1950	St Philip's Marsh
1951	St Philip's Marsh
1952	St Philip's Marsh; Cardiff East Dock (Sept.)
1953	Cardiff East Dock; Exeter (Sept.)
1954	Exeter
1955	St Blazey (Jan.)
1956	Swindon Works for LT

To London Transport 07.10.56
Returned to BR 29.09.61

Presumed scrapped 1961

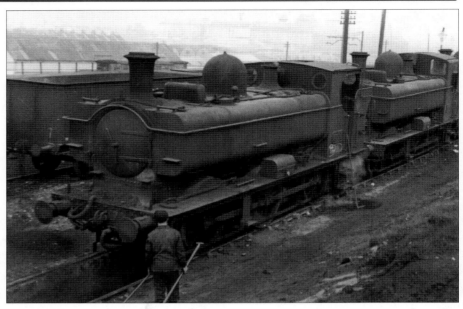

7711 at an unknown location c1947 in a grubby unkempt condition in company with another member of the class fitted with the later Collett style of cab which made them unsuitable for use on London Transport lines in that the cab was wider. *Great Western Trust*

7711 in BR black on test at Watford Tip in the early summer of 1957. *C. Foxall collection*

A recently purchased and repainted 7711 as L90 at Neasden in the summer of 1957. *Hugh Davies*

L90 [2] (7760)

Date	GWR/BR Shed allocation
1931	Built North British Locomotive Co., Glasgow.
1931	Into service January Laira
1932	Laira
1933	n/a
1934	Laira
1935	Laira
1936	Laira
1937	Laira
1938	Laira
1939	Laira; Old Oak Common (May)
1940	Old Oak Common
1941	Old Oak Common
1942	Old Oak Common
1943	Old Oak Common
1944	Old Oak Common
1945	Old Oak Common
1946	Old Oak Common
1947	Old Oak Common
1948	Old Oak Common
1949	Old Oak Common; Oxford (Sept.)
1950	Oxford
1951	Oxford
1952	Oxford
1953	Oxford
1954	Oxford
1955	Oxford
1956	Oxford
1957	Oxford
1958	Oxford
1959	Oxford
1960	Oxford
1961	Oxford; Wolverhampton Works (Sept.) for LT

To London Transport 14.11.61
Withdrawn 06.06.71

Originally sold to the Steel Breaking & Dismantling Co.

Then sold and preserved Tyseley Locomotive Works, Birmingham

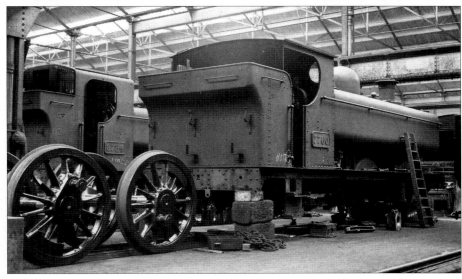

7760 undergoing a heavy overhaul at Swindon on the 26th March 1939. Its wheels are in the foreground and other parts are stripped for repair.
Roger Carpenter

7760 in early BR livery at Oxford in the late 1950s while shunting in the shed yard.
R. K. Blencowe collection

A well kept 7760, L90, at Watford Tip 23rd March 1969. *R. K. Blencowe collection*

L91 [1] (5752)

Date	GWR/BR Shed allocation
1929	Into service April Old Oak Common
1930	Old Oak Common
1931	Old Oak Common
1932	Old Oak Common
1933	n/a
1934	Old Oak Common to Southall (Dec.)
1935	Southall; Old Oak Common (May)
1936	Old Oak Common
1937	Old Oak Common
1938	Old Oak Common
1939	Old Oak Common
1940	Old Oak Common
1941	Old Oak Common; Didcot (Sept.)
1942	Didcot (with spark arrester plates)
1943	Didcot
1944	Didcot
1945	Didcot
1946	Didcot
1947	Didcot
1948	Didcot
1949	Didcot
1950	Didcot
1951	Didcot
1952	Didcot
1953	Didcot
1954	Didcot
1955	Didcot
1956	Didcot
1957	Didcot

To London Transport 25.02.57
Returned to BR 18.11.60

Scrapped Swansea

Great Western period views of 5752 have proved impossible to find but when at Didcot it was photographed frequently. *H. C. Casserley*

5752 fitted with spark arrester chimney in the early 1950s in company with large prairie tanks of the '61XX' class. At this date 5752 was shedded at Didcot and spark arresting chimneys were fitted to a number of locomotives there. *Great Western Trust*

L91 at Neasden on 7th June 1958 in ex-works LT red livery. *Rail Archive Stephenson*

L91 [2] (5757)

Date	GWR/BR Shed allocation
1929	Built GWR, Swindon
1929	Into service May Old Oak Common
1930	Old Oak Common
1931	Old Oak Common
1932	Old Oak Common
1933	n/a
1934	Old Oak Common
1935	Old Oak Common
1936	Old Oak Common
1937	Old Oak Common
1938	Old Oak Common
1939	Old Oak Common; St Philip's Marsh (July)
1940	St Philip's Marsh
1941	St Philip's Marsh
1942	St Philip's Marsh
1943	St Philip's Marsh
1944	St Philip's Marsh
1945	St Philip's Marsh
1946	St Philip's Marsh
1947	St Philip's Marsh; Westbury (April)
1948	Westbury; Frome (April); Westbury (Nov.)
1949	Westbury
1950	Westbury
1951	Westbury
1952	Westbury
1953	Westbury
1954	Westbury
1955	Westbury
1956	Westbury
1957	Westbury
1958	Westbury
1959	Westbury
1960	Westbury

To London Transport 18.11.60

Originally numbered L96, renumbered in 1961

Withdrawn 12.1969

Scrapped Neasden shed by Steel Breaking & Dismantling Company of Sheffield under contract 21.09.70.

5757 ahead of its future as it runs through Kensington Addison Road (Olympia) with a long freight for south London.
Great Western Trust

5757 on shed at Frome in company with a Collett cabbed sister September 1959.
photographer unknown

L91 at Lillie Bridge shed c1963 in clean condition awaiting its next turn of duty.
photographer unknown

L92 (5786)

Date	GWR/BR Shed allocation
1929	Built GWR, Swindon
1930	Into service January: Aberdare
1931	Aberdare
1932	Aberdare
1933	n/a
1934	Aberdare
1935	Aberdare
1936	Aberdare
1937	Aberdare
1938	Aberdare
1939	Aberdare
1940	Aberdare; Aberbeeg (May)
1941	Aberbeeg
1942	Aberbeeg
1943	Aberbeeg
1944	Aberbeeg; Tondu (July)
1945	Tondu; Aberbeeg (May)
1946	Aberbeeg
1947	Aberbeeg
1948	Aberbeeg
1949	Cardiff
1950	Cardiff
1951	Cardiff
1952	Cardiff
1953	Cardiff
1954	Cardiff
1955	Cardiff
1956	Cardiff
1957	Cardiff
1958	Cardiff

To London Transport 20.04.58
Withdrawn 03.10.69

Preserved	Worcester Locomotive Society. South Devon Railway

5786 at an unknown location in a grubby working condition c1935. *Great Western Trust*

5786 on shed at Tondu in mid 1950s. *Lens of Sutton Association*

L92 outside Neasden shed during the summer of 1968. *Kirk Martin*

L93 (7779)

Date	GWR/BR Shed allocation
1930	Built Armstrong-Whitworth, Newcastle
1930	Into service November Old Oak Common
1931	Southall (Jan.)
1932	Southall
1933	n/a
1934	Swindon Works; St Philip's Marsh
1935	St Philip's Marsh
1936	St Philip's Marsh
1937	St Philip's Marsh
1938	St Philip's Marsh
1939	St Philip's Marsh and Weston-super-M for occ. month
1940	St Philip's Marsh and Weston-super-M for occ. month
1941	St Philip's Marsh and Weston-super-M for occ. month
1942	St Philip's Marsh and Weston-super-M for occ. month
1943	St Philip's Marsh and Weston-super-M for occ. month
1944	St Philip's Marsh and Weston-super-M for occ. month
1945	St Philip's Marsh and Weston-super-M for occ. month
1946	St Philip's Marsh and Weston-super-M for occ. month
1947	St Philip's Marsh
1948	St Philip's Marsh
1949	St Philip's Marsh
1950	St Philip's Marsh
1951	St Philip's Marsh
1952	St Philip's Marsh; Barry (Sept.)
1953	Barry; Radyr (Dec.)
1954	Radyr
1955	Radyr
1956	Radyr
1957	Radyr
1958	Radyr; Swindon Works (June, July) for LT

To London Transport 05.10.58
Withdrawn 12.67

Scrapped Neasden shed by Steel Breaking & Dismantling Company of Sheffield under contract. 08.09.68

7779 at Southall shed in the early 1930s in need of a clean with its GWR lettering peeping through the grime. *Rail Archive Stephenson*

7779 heads a pick up freight at an unknown location c1951. *Great Western Trust*

L93 at Lillie Bridge c1965 while shunting the yard. *P. Fink*

L94 (7752)

Date	GWR/BR Shed allocation
1930	Built North British Locomotive Co., Glasgow
1930	Into service November Aberdare
1931	Aberdare
1932	Aberdare
1933	n/a
1934	Aberdare; Newport Ebbw (Aug.)
1935	Newport Ebbw
1936	Newport Ebbw
1937	Newport Ebbw
1938	Newport Ebbw
1939	Newport Ebbw
1940	Newport Ebbw
1941	Newport Ebbw
1942	Newport Ebbw
1943	Newport Ebbw; Aberbeeg (Aug.)
1944	Aberbeeg
1945	Aberbeeg
1946	Aberbeeg; Tondu (Nov.)
1947	Tondu
1948	Tondu
1949	Tondu
1950	Tondu
1951	Tondu; and stored (Dec.)
1952	Stored; Tondu (July)
1953	Tondu
1954	Tondu
1955	Tondu
1956	Tondu
1957	Tondu
1958	Tondu
1959	Tondu

To London Transport 01.11.59
Withdrawn 06.06.71

Preserved	Tyseley Locomotive Works, Birmingham

Images of 7752 in service whilst shedded in South Wales have proved difficult to find but it is seen here at Tondu shed on the 29th April 1951, sandwiched between two '66XX' 0-6-2Ts.
Great Western Trust

A portrait of L94 in the yard at Neasden. *R. A. Simpson, courtesy Colin Judge*

L94 in the top end of the yard at Neasden summer 1968. *Kirk Martin*

L95 (5764)

Date	GWR/BR Shed allocation
1929	Built GWR, Swindon
1929	Into service July
	Old Oak Common
1930	Old Oak Common
1931	Old Oak Common
1932	Old Oak Common
1933	n/a
1934	Old Oak Common
1935	Old Oak Common
1936	Old Oak Common
1937	Old Oak Common
1938	Old Oak Common
1939	Old Oak Common
1940	Old Oak Common
1941	Old Oak Common
1942	Old Oak Common
1943	Old Oak Common
1944	Old Oak Common
1945	Old Oak Common
1946	Old Oak Common
1947	Old Oak Common
1948	Old Oak Common
1949	Old Oak Common
1950	Old Oak Common
1951	Old Oak Common
1952	Old Oak Common
1953	Old Oak Common
1954	Old Oak Common
1955	Old Oak Common
1956	Old Oak Common
1957	Old Oak Common
1958	Old Oak Common
1959	Old Oak Common
1960	Old Oak Common

To London Transport 22.05.60
Withdrawn 19.06.71

Preserved   Severn Valley Railway

5764 in original condition at Old Oak Common shed c1935 on carriage pilot duties.
photographer unknown

5764 at Old Oak Common shed c1955 in company with a '97XX' condenser pannier which would have worked the Smithfield meat trains over the northern part of the Circle Line via Paddington and Kings Cross. *Lens of Sutton Association*

L95 at Watford Tip c1970 in well worn LT livery. *C. Foxall collection*

L96 (7741)

Date	GWR/BR Shed allocation
1930	Built North British Locomotive Co., Glasgow
1930	Into service February Gloucester; Bullo Pill (Aug.)
1931	Bullo Pill; Gloucester (April)
1932	Gloucester
1933	n/a
1934	Gloucester
1935	Gloucester
1936	Gloucester
1937	Gloucester; Hereford (May); Gloucester (August)
1938	Gloucester; Kidderminster (October)
1939	Kidderminster; Gloucester (May)
1940	Gloucester
1941	Gloucester
1942	Gloucester
1943	Gloucester
1944	Gloucester
1945	Gloucester
1946	Gloucester
1947	Gloucester
1948	Gloucester
1949	Gloucester
1950	Gloucester
1951	Gloucester
1952	Gloucester; Lydney (March)
1953	Lydney
1954	Lydney
1955	Lydney
1956	Lydney
1957	Lydney
1958	Lydney
1959	Lydney
1960	Lydney
1961	Lydney; Wolverhampton Works (Sept.) for LT

To London Transport 14.11.61
Withdrawn 12.66

Scrapped Neasden shed by Steel Breaking & Dismantling Company of Sheffield under contract. 21.09.67

7741 in early British Rail days but still carrying its faded Great Western livery. Whilst the location is not recorded from the allocation list it is likely to be at Gloucester. *courtesy Paul Karau*

7741 at Lydney shed in late BR livery. *J. Davenport/Initial photos*

L96 in a reasonably clean state on Neasden shed. Notice the higher positioning of London Transport on the tank sides. *Colour Rail*

L97 (7749)

Date	GWR/BR Shed allocation
1930	Built North British Locomotive Co., Glasgow
1930	Into service March Westbury
1931	Westbury
1932	Westbury
1933	n/a
1934	Westbury (alternating with Frome & Salisbury)
1935	Swindon (Jan.), alternating with Andover
1936	Swindon, alternating with Andover & Chippenham
1937	Swindon
1938	Swindon
1939	Swindon Works; Westbury (March)
1940	Westbury
1941	Westbury; Salisbury (May); St Philip's Marsh (Dec.)
1942	St Philip's Marsh and Weston-super-M for occ. month
1943	St Philip's Marsh and Weston-super-M for occ. month
1944	St Philip's Marsh and Weston-super-M for occ. month
1945	St Philip's Marsh and Weston-super-M for occ. month
1946	St Philip's Marsh and Weston-super-M for occ. month
1947	St Philip's Marsh and Weston-super-M for occ. month
1948	St Philip's Marsh
1949	St Philip's Marsh
1950	St Philip's Marsh
1951	St Philip's Marsh
1952	St Philip's Marsh
1953	St Philip's Marsh
1954	St Philip's Marsh; Weymouth (Aug.) St P M (Nov.)
1955	St Philip's Marsh
1956	St Philip's Marsh
1957	St Philip's Marsh
1958	St Philip's Marsh
1959	St Philip's Marsh
1960	St Philip's Marsh
1961	St Philip's Marsh
1962	St Philip's Marsh; to LT July

To London Transport 11.08.62
Withdrawn 09.68

Scrapped Neasden shed by Steel Breaking & Dismantling Company of Sheffield under contract. 29.01.70

7749 on shed at an unknown location c1935 in original condition.
Great Western Trust

7749 hauls a train of wagons at Bristol Docks c1955 on dock shunting duties.
Lens of Sutton Association

L97 stands in Neasden Yard summer 1968.
Kirk Martin

L98 (7739)

Date	GWR/BR Shed allocation
1930	Built North British Locomotive Co., Glasgow
1930	Into service February Swansea East Dock
1931	Neath & Brecon (Oct.); Neath (Dec.)
1932	alternating Neath; Neath & Brecon; and Glyn Neath
1933	n/a
1934	Neath & Brecon; Neath (Nov.)
1935	alternating Neath; Neath & Brecon; and Glyn Neath
1936	alternating Neath; Neath & Brecon; and Glyn Neath
1937	alternating Neath; Neath & Brecon; and Glyn Neath
1938	alternating Neath; Neath & Brecon; and Glyn Neath
1939	alternating Neath; Neath & Brecon; and Glyn Neath
1940	alternating Neath; Neath & Brecon; and Glyn Neath
1941	alternating Neath; Neath & Brecon; and Glyn Neath
1942	Neath; Neath & Brecon (Feb.)
1943	alternating Neath; Neath & Brecon; and Glyn Neath
1944	alternating Neath; Neath & Brecon
1945	alternating Neath; Neath & Brecon; and Glyn Neath
1946	alternating Neath; Neath & Brecon; and Glyn Neath
1947	alternating Neath; Neath & Brecon; and Glyn Neath
1948	alternating Neath; Neath & Brecon
1949	Neath & Brecon
1950	Neath & Brecon
1951	Neath & Brecon
1952	Neath & Brecon
1953	Neath & Brecon
1954	Neath & Brecon
1955	Neath & Brecon
1956	Neath & Brecon
1957	Neath & Brecon; Neath (March)
1958	Neath
1959	Neath
1960	Neath
1961	Neath
1962	Neath; Wolverhampton Works (August) for LT

To London Transport 04.12.62
Withdrawn 11.68

Scrapped Neasden shed by Steel Breaking & Dismantling Company of Sheffield under contract. 29.01.70

7739 at Neath shed 30th June 1957.   *R. J. Brockley/Initial Photos*

7739 at Neath, 29th April 1951.   *Great Western Trust*

L98 outside Neasden shed,   *Kirk Martin*

L99 (7715)

Date	GWR/BR Shed allocation
1930	Built Kerr Stuart, Stoke on Trent
1930	Into service June St Blazey
1931	St Blazey
1932	St Blazey
1933	n/a
1934	St Blazey
1935	Swindon Works; Laira (Feb.)
1936	Laira; St Blazey (March)
1937	St Blazey
1938	St Blazey
1939	St Blazey
1940	St Blazey; Laira (March)
1941	Laira; St Blazey (October)
1942	St Blazey
1943	St Blazey
1944	St Blazey
1945	St Blazey
1946	St Blazey
1947	St Blazey
1948	St Blazey
1949	St Blazey
1950	St Blazey
1951	St Blazey
1952	St Blazey
1953	St Blazey
1954	St Blazey
1955	St Blazey
1956	St Blazey
1957	St Blazey
1958	St Blazey; Store (Dec.)
1959	St Blazey
1960	St Blazey
1961	St Blazey
1962	St Blazey; Duffryn Yard (Jan.)
1963	Duffryn Yard; Sdn Works (Feb.); LT (April)

To London Transport 24.06.63
Withdrawn 01.01.70

Preserved	London Railway Preservation Society. Buckinghamshire Railway Centre, Quainton Road

7715 on a china clay train near St Blazey in Cornwall on the 7th July 1949 looking very tired in its post war green livery. *Great Western Trust*

7715 at St Blazey on a china clay train 22nd July 1957. *J. Davenport/Initial Photos*

L99 by Neasden Power Station cooling tower. Note ex-LMS 20-ton brake van next to mineral wagons – summer 1968. *Kirk Martin*

Hopper Ballast Wagons

These 20-ton ballast hoppers were numbered HW.400-437 of which 400 to 434 were built in three batches by the Gloucester Railway Carriage & Wagon Co.; seven in 1935, five in 1938, and the rest in 1951. In 1965 three further wagons were acquired from British Railways. All were fitted with conventional drawgear and the Underground's Ward couplers, the use of which meant that the buffers had to be retractable.

In the top view four of the 20-ton hoppers can be seen together at Lillie Bridge. On the left and below are some of the builder's official views including a test of ballast spreading from the side and bottom doors.

G. Moon & Gloucestershire Archives

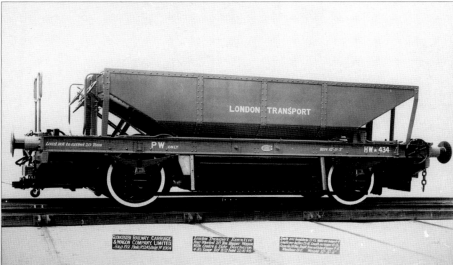

APPENDIX TWO
ENGINEERING WAGONS

Presented here, mainly for the benefit of modellers, is a small selection of engineering department wagons which were used in conjunction with the panniers. Greater details of these wagons can be found in *Workhorses of the Underground* by J. Graeme Bruce published in 1987.

Top right: A 10-ton ballast wagon which also had the facility to be converted into a flat wagon. They were built by the GRC&WCo. in 1935. Again they were fitted with both forms of coupling and hinged buffers which could be swung upwards. *Gloucestershire Archives*

Lower Right: The small ballast wagons survived in use well into the 1970s as seen here at Lillie Bridge where one had been converted to carry a water tank and numbered TW.740. In this instance the conventional drawgear is in use with the buffers down for coupling to the pannier and the Ward coupling with buffers folded back for coupling to the ballast hopper. *G. Moon*

Below: By far the largest number of open/ flat wagons were 30-ton capacity bogie 50ft vehicles first ordered in 1931. These could be used as open wagons for ballast or, with the sides removed, for rails or sleepers which made them extremely versatile. The wagon seen here was built by GRC&WCo. as part of a batch of thirty-one wagons ordered in 1951. Gloucester had supplied such wagons since 1935 and continued to do so until 1959. *Gloucestershire Archives*

A further selection of opens, flats and rail wagons starting at the top with F.376 one of the 30-ton open/flat wagons and one of two built at Acton Works in 1958. Below that is F.332 built by Gloucester in 1937 and seen at Lillie Bridge with a tank in one section which has the side boards fitted and containers in the open section. A further builder's photograph is on the right showing details of the couplings complete with safety side chains. Finally below is a rail wagon, RW.453. These were longer than the flat wagons as they were required to carry 60ft lengths of rail and had a capacity of 20 tons.

G. Moon & Gloucestershire Archives

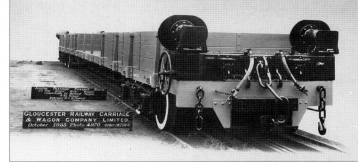

Above: Three special cable wagons were built by Gloucester and delivered in 1940. They were numbered CW.1050-1052 and ran as a close coupled rake. What is uncertain is whether originally they were intended only to have Ward couplings or whether this is the middle wagon of the rake. Later views of them in service show that the outer wagons were fitted with standard RCH couplings, hinged buffers and Ward couplers.

Gloucestershire Archives

Right & below: To end with a selection of brake vans. B.584 is one of the six vans acquired in 1962 and built at the Ashford Carriage & Wagon Works of British Railways. The two images below show Hurst, Nelson of Motherwell built vans supplied in 1935. Note the position of the guard's ducket varies on either side. *G. Moon & Ben Pope collection*

ACKNOWLEDGEMENTS

John Scott-Morgan and Kirk Martin have worked closely together on this immensely rewarding project. John has provided the historical survey, as well as some of his own memories, while Kirk has added to his own experience working at Neasden and Lillie Bridge by contacting a range of people who worked on, followed, and photographed these true survivors of the final years of steam traction in Britain.

A work of this nature would not have been possible without the images taken by the photographers and thus the authors give their deepest gratitude to Gordon Wells, Geoff Plumb and Keith Lawrence. For first-hand recollections of working with the locomotives thanks are due to Harry Robinson and Ron Head who also supplied photographs, for recollections of the last night run many thanks to Ken Mumford.

Others who have freely provided images from their collections are Jim Connor, A. Delicata, Philip Fink, Clive Foxall, Adrian Garner, Keith Harwood, Kevin McCormack, G. Moon, Mike Morant, Ben Pope, Keith Robertson, R. C. Stumpf, P. Watson, Frank Dumbleton and the Great Western Trust, and the Lens of Sutton Association. Special thanks to Andy Sturt who supplied an image all the way from Australia. Other individual photographers are credited where due under the photographs supplied.

Thanks are also due to Oliver Green of the LT Museum for checking the proofs and providing illustrations and to his staff in the library and photographic archive; Emma Theophilus-Wright at Transport for London Group Archives; John Copsey for the supply of the GWR/BR allocations; Paul Karau for the '57XX' works drawings, L. Bowles for locomotive information, and Gloucestershire Archives for images from the Gloucester Railway Carriage & Wagon Co. collection.

We should also like to express our gratitude to our publishers, in particular to Ian Pope for tidying up the original manuscript and for studying the photographs far too closely and thus raising several interesting questions. To Clare Pope our thanks for proof reading the finished work.

To any we may have missed who have assisted in this venture our apologies.

With a wisp of steam escaping from its safety valves L98 simmers on shed awaiting its next turn of duty whilst a sister locomotive stands at rest in the background – Lillie Bridge summer 1968. *Kirk Martin*

With the panniers gone from London Transport all that is left are memories and the photographic record. The Ghosts in the Night are now just that, a shadowy recollection. How apt then to finish with this image of L90 casting its shadow into the fields whilst returning from Watford in January 1970. *Ron Head*